Contents

The Future of Childhood

Alliance for Childhood

Articles for the Brussels Conference,
Rights to Children – a Bridge to the Future
11-14 October, 2000

Edited by Christopher Clouder,
Sally Jenkinson, Martin Large

Hawthorn Press

Published by Hawthorn Press, Hawthorn House, 1 Lansdown Lane, Stroud, Gloucestershire, GL5 1BJ, UK
Tel: (01453) 757040 Fax: (01453) 751138
www.hawthornpress.com
for the Alliance for Childhood, Kidbrooke Park, Forest Row, East Sussex, RH18 5JA
Tel: (01342) 822115

Cover image by Christiane Bryan
Cover design by Patrick Roe, Southgate Solutions, Stroud, Gloucestershire
Typesetting by Frances Fineran, Hawthorn Press, Stroud, Gloucestershire
Printed in the UK by Redwood Books, Trowbridge, Wiltshire

British Library Cataloguing in Publication Data applied for

ISBN 1 903458 10 2

Introduction

Christopher Clouder

There is an old Chinese proverb that runs 'If you plan for a year, plant rice. If you plan for ten years, plant trees. If you plan for a hundred years, educate your children.' This reminds us of the fact that the way we bring up and educate our children has effects that are of a nature that are longer term than we normally assume, and in our globalised world we should become even more conscious of this. As active adults and educators, in the broadest sense of the term, we are continually in the process of not only creating the future world for our own children but also for many generations to come.

At the beginning of the 19th century educational reformers, such as Ellen Key in Sweden, envisaged that it would be the century of childhood. It was believed that the value of childhood would be generally appreciated and seen as a common asset for humankind and that, by keeping children in a sort of paradisiacal protected garden, their healthy and happy future would be automatically assured. However history was to turn out differently, and at the beginning of the present century we find ourselves in a world where vast numbers of children still live in a harsh and hostile world. Many children face impoverishment, abuse, inadequate healthcare, violence and starvation. According to the United Nations Children's Fund, 650 million children are living in extreme poverty and this number is growing. Very many others feel the consequences of war and social disintegration.

Yet in the more affluent parts of the globe there are also other threats to the right to have a balanced and stress-free childhood. Commercialisation can place great pressure on children – and consequently on family life – when they are targeted as a vulnerable part of society and taught the habits of unlimited consumerism. Electronic media are seen as educational panaceas without enough consideration as to how they really affect young children emotionally and physically. Evidence is beginning to be published that suggests that such media should be approached with great caution with the very young. In many countries the mental health of very young children is becoming a cause of concern

In a society where there is pressure on both parents to work, safe and understanding childcare facilities are vitally important. This is too often not the case and children then suffer the deprivation of the loving care they need to develop in a balanced manner. More and more children, whose behaviour is seen as anti-social or uncontrolled, are being treated with drugs, such as Ritalin, yet we do not know the long-term consequences of such dependency.

It is frequently remarked upon that children are losing the ability to play and to exercise themselves healthily through movement, and this too will affect their adult behaviour and well-being. This list is long. There are, of course, many children who are able enjoy their childhoods and are well nurtured through these years. But, in a technological environment where we can achieve so much, the fact that there are many millions who do not is becoming increasingly irresponsible and eventually unforgivable.

There are many organisations devoted to the cause of children and through their determined endeavours they have proved profoundly effective over the years. Yet why do so many children still face a disadvantageous and potentially harmful daily reality? A possible answer lies not just in creating yet another organisation but in connecting the individuals already concerned: activists, teachers, parents, medical practitioners, social workers, politicians and researchers – whole organisations – cooperating with the sense of a combined purpose.

Hence the founding of the **Alliance for Childhood.** Its purpose is to bring about a sense of colleagueship in facing these dilemmas, so that a concerted effort can be made and nobody who is concerned need feel they are crying in wilderness of inactivity and hopelessness. We now live in a global economy where we are affected be decisions taken very remotely from our immediate communities. We should look at the plight of the world's children in a similar way if we are to make an impression.

Working across boundaries of historical prejudice, national intolerance and misunderstanding, competitive market practices and economic expediency, we can, together, work to honour and appreciate the greatest gift we can be given – our children and their childhood – and the love they elicit and give.

We want to create something like the ethical pressure group **Amnesty International** on behalf of childhood, so that eventually attitudes will change, and a greater understanding can come about as to what childhood means and what it has meant to all of us. We could accordingly act with greater responsibility and insight. A romantic vision, perhaps, but it is clear that the pressures against a good quality and nourishing childhood are growing for too many children. A stand must now be taken.

Each culture and country will have its own particular priorities, strengths as well as deficiencies. By working internationally we can share expertise and enthusiasm to help each other, find mutual support and sources of courage and energy. With an interested respect for each other's endeavours and viewpoints we can widen our own horizons to become more supportive of each other.

The gifts of a real childhood are creativity, wonder and imagination and, by extending these qualities into our adulthood, we can help those future generations who will be born into an increasingly complex and fragile world to enjoy their right to childhood. We have to take practical steps. By becoming a partner in the Alliance you can help us explore what these steps may be and become colleagues in implementing them. The conference and this collection of papers are initial and experimental steps in this direction.

September 2000

Foreword

Martin Large

The Future of Childhood is a collection of articles and papers generously offered by a cross section of Brussels 2000 conference contributors. The purpose of the book is to deepen and stimulate dialogues during the conference, and to share the articles with others afterwards as a resource.

Tight deadlines made it hard for some conference contributors to write an article. We were also unable to get permission, or the text on disc or e-mail on time, for other articles which therefore sadly had to be left out. There may be some errors in references or consistency, and articles were only lightly edited because of time constraints. In the end, we had 5 weeks to edit, design, typeset, print and get the book to Brussels. Hence, the order of articles in the book was determined by when we received them, rather than by a logical progression.

However, if enough people offer appropriate follow up articles to the Conference by the end of December 2000 and if there are enough firm advance orders (see the last page of this book for an order form), a Proceedings book can be considered if viable.

I also apologise to non-English speakers and readers for this English language book for the Conference: time and resources were limiting factors here. However, individuals, magazines, publishers and professional groups are welcome to contact the authors of the respective articles direct if they want to get permission to have any articles translated and reproduced.

Our thanks and acknowledgements to: Sally Jenkinson and Joan Almon for their help in choosing and suggesting articles; Christopher Clouder, Oona Murphy, Christiane Dawson and Juergen Flinspach of the Alliance for their support; respective contributors, organisations and publishers for their kind permission to reproduce their articles in this book.

The Future of Childhood is published by Hawthorn Press for the Alliance for Childhood. We have included this book in our Early Years Series, which has the purpose of 'Respecting the right to childhood'. Or to echo Cathy Nutbrown, 'How are we giving due respect to children in the 21st century?'

1. With due respect: 'making sure' for childhoods in the 21st Century

Dr. Cathy Nutbrown

My inclusion of children's rights in my own research agenda was born, not only of my conviction that children's rights raised important issues in their own right, but also because I believed that the early years of education in England presented a yet to be developed arena for work on children's rights. Remarkably few early childhood educators know of, and fewer still are conversant with, the United Nations Convention for the Rights of the Child. There is a number of reasons for this but the chief difficulties lie first in the culture – in England – of 'rights' as contestable and second – but related – in the lack of professional development experiences for educators in England to learn of and think about international issues in early childhood in general and early education in particular. My own work is driven by the commitment that children, from birth, must be enabled to experience their rights and we must bear some additional responsibility for children so that they can experience their rights. Gradually adults can teach children about the responsibilities that must attach to rights and help them to learn how to assume and shoulder the responsibilities of citizenship. Some still argue that young children must not be endowed with rights because they cannot shoulder the attached responsibility; but this is a position only of those who seek continually to deny children the citizenship that is rightfully theirs.

I want to encourage adults who live and work with children to address some difficult and penetrating questions which require us to reflect on our own thinking and practice, our politics and personal policies, our own beliefs and values.

Views of Childhood

The famous and talented sculptor Barbara Hepworth wrote:

Perhaps what one wants to say is formed in childhood and the rest of one's life is spent in trying to say it.

Her words affirm, for me, the importance of childhood as a time of thinking, formation, foundation and crucial beginnings. Childhood is a time when the path of one's life is influenced and perhaps the course set. It can be a time of active decision making, engaging relentlessly with minute-to-minute experiences, and making one's mark upon the world, a vital time in the life of every human being. It is a time, as Christian Schiller might have said for *Educaré* a time to… *cherish the growth of the young.*

Another view of children and childhood is still held by some individuals, indeed by some societies Such a view holds children as passive recipients of knowledge, as necessary burdens, as 'adults in waiting', 'adults in the making', 'unfinished', 'not quite there yet'. Indeed I once heard an academic speak of children as 'emergent human beings'. Hazareesingh, et al (1989) – considered this when they wrote:

This concept of the child as an 'unfinished' adult shifts the focus away from the child's own intentions, attachments, and strivings – which might in fact open up many learning horizons for the adult, on to an end-product notion of adulthood which is unwisely equated with 'achieved knowledge'. It might be said that this represents a specifically western, 'rationalist' approach to both childhood and learning which by separating the mind from the heart, effectively denies the essential unity of the child.

(Hazareesingh, et al 1989, p.18)

The 'adults in waiting' construction of childhood devalues children as capable learners. It underpins the creation of narrow curricula and systems of educating which are built on the transmission of pre-ordained, pre-packed nuggets of knowledge. Such perspectives on childhood omit children who can use their powers as thinkers from the learning equation and, too often, denies their humanity. Kakar (1981) described a view of childhood in some Indian Chinese and African cultures as *a fully meaningful world-in-itself with its own way of being, seeing, and feeling,* and further argued that

Indian philosophies, for instance, stress that the child should not simply be 'brought up': there is an accompanying responsibility for the adult to enter into the child's mode of experiencing the world

(Kakar, 1981 p.18)

Such is the case in some European Countries too, in Denmark for instance the Children's Welfare Commission set four goals for a policy on children:

- to respect the child as an individual in the family and in society;
- to give the child a central position in the life of grown-ups;
- to promote – in a wider sense – the physical conditions in which children grow up;

- to promote equal opportunities, in the conditions of life of children, both in a material and in a cultural sense.

(Villen, 1993)

When I visited two kindergartens in Copenhagen as part of an OMEP (Organisation Mondiale pour l'éducation Préscholaire) seminar in the mid 1990s I saw children who were valued as young citizens and adults who were respected for the work they did with those children. This was evident in beautiful and exciting gardens with ropes hanging from trees, huge sandy areas with planks of wood, crates and tyres for make believe play on a large scale. Garden sheds which were child size so that children could get a bike, a pram or whatever, when **they** wanted it, and be responsible for replacing it after use. Adults were valued to the extent that their staff space, (kitchen and rest room) were beautiful too – matching cups and plates, thought out colour schemes, comfortable and matching chairs, space to relax with colleagues, to discuss and to work. I was told that to be a Pedagogue in Denmark (Kindergarten Worker) was a much sought after and valued job for men and women. Similar attention to the importance of the environment is visible in the preschools of Reggio Emilia (Abbott and Nutbrown forthcoming), where the environment is central to the values of those who work in communities of learning with young children, articulated by Malaguzzi – the founder of the Reggio Approach who said:

It is indisputable that schools should have the right to their own environment, their architecture, their own conceptualisation and utilization of spaces, forms, and functions.

(Malaguzzi 1996:40)

Taking a glance, internationally, of views of childhood and adults' visions for them provides us with perspectives which can challenge our own (often uninterrogated) culturally and socially constructed views of childhood. In China, for example, the 'one child per family' policy makes for a very different attitude towards childhood. Such a policy, it could be argued, can – en masse – deny children the experience of siblings, overwhelm 'only children' with adult attention from grandparents, parents and other close family members, and elevate a single child in a family to a position of reverence. In Trinidad and Tobago there is still a culture within many families of physical punishment of young children, though the pioneering work of SERVOL is enabling early childhood educators in preschools to develop alternative strategies to support children in managing their behaviour without resorting to violence. In Sweden the 'My Rights' project began with work in 1985 and now involves some 50 NGOs combining to produce information for children to inform them of their rights (Backstrom 1997). Societies world wide place many demands upon children (Durkheim 1994), and there is a range of perspectives on children's lives and children's rights in different social contexts (Mayall 1994), but the UN convention provides for us the opportunity of speaking a common language, working towards internationally articulated goals, for children within their own distinctive cultures and communities.

So society's and individual's views of children influence the ways in which they are cared for, provided for and educated in their early years. It is important to question the seriousness with which the UK considers its children, and more than that, how does the European Community view its children and what visions for their future does the Europe of the 21st Century hold for its youngest citizens? Does a country, a community, respect children as people, citizens, able learners, powerful thinkers, feeling human beings?

Equally important are the questions to be asked of educators. Do educators watch children's actions and listen to their voices with *Wide Eyes and Open Minds?* (Nutbrown 1996) or are children seen as 'adults-in-waiting' with no real rights, not yet real people, not yet able to think for themselves, no rightful place in the world? Do educators decide *for* children, working with their eyes closed and minds narrow to the view that they are working with powerful and able people, however small and however young they may be? How do adults 'make sure' of childhoods in the 21st Century?

We must recognise the motivations which drive us to work with and for children and ensure that children's interests are served first and not, as Oldman (1995) argues to be the case, allow this work to become dominated by the interests of adults.

In England and Wales, much has been written about what children should be able to do when they are five years old. The School Curriculum and Assessment Authority issued for consultation in September 1995 a document describing the *Desirable Outcomes* of *preschool education* (SCAA 1995). This indicated, and was shaped by, particular positions and assumptions on what childhood is and what, at a certain stage in childhood, should be accomplished. This importance of this document was acknowledged both by the chief executive of SCAA who in the accompanying letter wrote: *'This is an important consultation. There is a lot at stake for all children...'* and by Sir Ron Dearing, who, in the foreword to the document said:

In this consultation we are taking the first step on a matter of much importance to children themselves and for the future of education. The quality of children's early education influences their development and achievement.

(SCAA 1995)

Views of childhood are important when policy decisions affecting children's childhoods and futures are being taken and it is interesting, (perhaps disturbing), to note that when adults try to make plans for children and the future they sometimes cast blame in the wrong place. An article *'What a mess to clear up!'*, reporting the launch of the SCAA Preschool Education consultation document began like this:

The hordes of four year olds piling into nurseries and playgroups this week are far too busy with the paint and glue and sand and water to worry about the mess they are causing. But Gillian Shepherd has a lot of clearing up to do.

(Guardian 12 .9.95)

They, the children, had caused no *mess* at all, but this characterisation of children as the *problem* is an important one to note. That same article forecast a fierce *debate* between *progressives* and *traditionalists*. Well, perhaps this is one situation where we can confidently say that *traditional nursery education is progressive.* The *traditions* of learning through play and observation of children inherited from the work of those such as Froebel, Montessori and developed in the UK by the Macmillans and Isaacs are the very strands of nursery education which are now being cast as *child centred* and *progressive.*

The book *Respectful Educators – Capable Learners* (Nutbrown 1996) represented a hope for further progression in the development of educational provision for young children. The contributors highlighted what was good in current practices. They discussed the place of, and progress in, children's rights through topics including: inspection; equality; curriculum, observation and assessment; special educational needs; training early childhood workers; work with parents; and play. The final chapter discussed argued that children's best interests would be served if provision for the youngest children were examined to see how well it respected the rights of children and enabled them to experience the quality of education and care which is enshrined in Article 29, and other articles in the Convention.

Article 29

a The development of the child's personality, talents and mental and physical abilities to their fullest potential:

b the development of respect for human rights and fundamental freedoms, and for the principles enshrined in the charter of the United Nations

c The development of respect for the child's parents, his or her own cultural identity, language and values, for the national values of the country in which the child is living, the country from which he or she may originate, and for civilisations different from his or her own

d the preparation of the child for responsible life in a free society, in the spirit of understanding, peace, tolerance, equality of sexes, and friendship among all peoples, ethnic, national and religious groups and persons of indigenous origin;

e the development of respect for the natural environment.

Drawing on Article 29 it posed a series of questions for educators to debate in relation to their own work with children. I pose more questions for educators and policy makers to ponder on how they will make sure of childhood, with due respect for children of the 21st Century:

20 questions for childhoods of the 21st Century

- How does the provision foster the development of individuals, their personality, their talents, their thinking and their actions to the fullest?

- Do educators observe and discuss the personalities and preferences of the children they work with – babies, toddlers, and older children?

- Do the children work on challenging problems?

- Do children confront issues which puzzle and bother them?

- How can a service for children foster healthy hearts and minds?

- Do educators challenge children to think or do they train children to conform?

- What does a respectful service for children look like and feel like?

- To what extent do educators foster respect for human rights, freedom of choice and principles of dignity, individualism and mutual respect enshrined in the charter?

- Is difference and diversity recognised and celebrated?

- Does the nursery teach children about their rights and enable them to discuss what having 'rights' means to them?

- What does a respectful early childhood curriculum look like, feel like?

- Are children helped to understand that they have the right to make choices?

- Are children encouraged to assert their right to express themselves, their love, their likes, their fears, their dislikes, their wants, their hates, their feelings?

- How is respect shown to parents?

- How are children encouraged to be proud of who they are, what they look like, how they speak and to respect the differences of others?

- Is diversity of language, culture and identity valued, or does one culture and one language dominate?

- Is there a climate of co-operation and equality?

- Do staff value children's rights to challenge, question and assert them?

- Are children taught how they might assert themselves without aggression?

- Do children's outdoor experiences foster an appreciation, understanding and respect for the natural environment?

These difficult and searching questions might support those who want to develop their provision for young children in ways which more fully support and realise their rights.

There are obligations on Governments, yes, but there are responsibilities for every adult citizen too, making sure that childhood is the responsibility of every adult. In 1996 *Respectful educators – capable learners* (Nutbrown 1996) looked forward to how things might be if, as individuals and as a nation, we took further account of the need to respect children, their capabilities and their rights and help them to reach their potential. Some five years later though, it remains the case that out of a conference audience of 200 early childhood educators, ten might raise their hands when asked if they have heard of the UN convention on the rights of the child. Fewer admit to being conversant with the contents of the Convention. There is still much to do to inform early childhood educators about the rights of the child and even more to do to ensure that they know enough about children's rights and the UN Convention to work within it.

Respect must be nurtured in children for they are capable and quick learners, they will learn the messages and values adults transmit to them. Respectful educators will ensure that diversity and difference is celebrated and that children are empowered to 'BE' themselves as well as learn BEside others.

Early education worldwide needs to focus on development for living which – in the words of the UN Convention – help children to *'foster respect, human rights, freedom of choice, and principles of dignity, individualism and mutual respect'*. There remains the challenge – to work with due respect with young children and their families into the 21st Century and to make sure of childhoods.

Cathy Nutbrown began her career as a teacher of young children and has since worked in a range of settings and roles with parents, teachers, and early childhood educators. Her research interests include children's early learning and development, their literacy, assessment, children's rights and work with parents. She is currently Lecturer in Education at The Department of Educational Studies at The University of Sheffield, where she directs the distance learning MA in Early Childhood Education.

Cathy has written many articles on early education, literacy and assessment. Her books include *Respectful Educators – Capable Learners: children's rights in early education* (PCP 1996), and recently *Recognising Early Literacy Development – Assessing Children's Achievements* (PCP 1997), and *Threads of Thinking –* (1999) which examines children's learning in the context of current policies. Cathy is committed to finding ways of working 'with respect' with young children, and sees the concept of quality in the context of what it means to develop curriculum and pedagogy in the early years with the ambition of working in a climate of 'respectful education'.

Contact:

Dr. Cathy Nutbrown,
The University of Sheffield, Department of Educational Studies,
The Education Building, 388 Glossop Road,
Sheffield, S10 2JA

Tel: 0114 222 8139
E-mail: c.e.nutbrown@sheffield.ac.uk

References

Backstrom, K. (1997) 'The significance of the UN Convention on the rights of the child to children in preschool and school' Paper given at the 22nd International Montessori Congress 'The Child and Communication' July 22-27 1997 www.ilu.uu.se/ilu/montessori/index/htm

Durkheim, E. (1994) Education and society, in A. Giddens (1996) *Emile Durkheim: Selected Writings Cambridge: Cambridge University Press*

Hazareesingh, S., Simms, K. and Anderson, P. (1989) *Educating the whole child – A holistic Approach to Education in the Early Years,* Building Blocks Early Years Project/Save the Children, Equality Learning Centre, 357 Holloway Road, London N7 6PA

Kakar, S. (1981) *The Inner World. A Psycho-analytic Study of Childhood and Society in India* Oxford University Press, New Delhi.

Malaguzzi, L. (1996) The right to environment. In Filippini, T, and Vecchi, V. (1996) *The Hundred Languages of Children: the exhibit* Reggio Emilia: Reggio Children

Mayall, B (ed) (1994) *Children's Childhoods Observed and Experienced* Falmer Press, London

Oldman, D. (1994) Childhood as a mode of production, in B. Mayall (ed) (1994) *Children's Childhoods Observed and Experienced* Falmer Press, London

School Curriculum and Assessment Authority (SCAA) (1996) *Nursery Education – desirable outcomes for children's learning on entering compulsory education* SCAA and DfEE, London

UN (1989) *Convention on the Rights of the Child* New York, United Nations

Villen, K. (1993) Pre-school education in Denmark, in T. David (ed) *Educational Provision for our Youngest Children: European Perspectives* Paul Chapman, London

2. The Right to Choose and Learn

Wendy Scott

Introduction

The focus of this paper is on how early years professionals can promote the United Nations Convention on the Rights of the Child through the curriculum they plan and provide in their work settings. Children are able to make choices, develop responsible attitudes and become independent learners from a very young age provided that adults ensure that an appropriate curriculum is negotiated within a well-planned environment. Teachers and other practitioners need knowledge about children's capabilities, and respect both for their powers and their rights to growing autonomy.

The curriculum involves the learning experiences on offer to the children, unintended as well as planned. For under fives, it is essential that adults retain the flexibility to respond to spontaneous events as well as to anticipated possibilities. Staff need to be aware of the underlying purposes children may be exploring as they refine their skills and concepts alongside the acquisition of knowledge. It is significant that the approach to curriculum endorsed by educational theory and research reinforces the principles embodied in the Convention.

Article 42 makes it clear that the state has an obligation to make the principles and provisions of the Convention on the Rights of the Child widely known by appropriate and active means. The British government's Select Committee on Education, in its initial report on the education of children under five, published in 1989 (DES, 1989), and its restatement published in 1994 (HC Select Committee, 1994), has taken a firm stance that is consistent with our responsibilities as signatories of the Convention.

'Starting with Quality', the Report of the Committee of Inquiry into the Quality of the Educational Experience Offered to 3- and 4-year-olds (the Rumbold Report: DES, 1990) laid down a strong foundation that is entirely compatible with the articles of the Convention. This detailed guidance, confirmed by cumulative research findings and further authoritative reports (National Commission on Education, 1993; Ball, 1994), provides a clear agenda for progress which must be implemented by adults who have in-depth knowledge of children's capabilities and profound respect for their powers. There are indications that the current inquiry into early learning by the Parliamentary Select Committee for Education and Employment will re-state earlier findings, and reinforce them through reference to a specially commissioned review of evidence from developmental psychology and brain research (Blakemore 2000).

Theory, research, curriculum and the UN Convention on Children's Rights

The most relevant articles of the Convention for this perspective on children's entitlement concern each child's right to express an opinion and to have that opinion taken into account, and the linked right to freedom of expression (articles 12 and 13). Article 28 highlights the importance of ensuring that discipline is administered in a manner consistent with the child's human dignity, and emphasises the need to encourage international co-operation in facilitating access to modern teaching methods. Article 29 deals explicitly with the recognition that education should be directed at 'the development of the child's personality, talents and mental and physical abilities to their fullest potential' and 'the preparation of the child for responsible life in a free society'. These phrases are echoed in the Education Reform Act 1988 in England and Wales, which states that 'the curriculum must... promote the spiritual, moral, cultural, mental, physical development of pupils at the school and of society, and prepare pupils for the opportunities, responsibilities and experiences of adult life'.

The statutory National Curriculum does not apply to children below statutory school age. However, the Early Years Curriculum Group (1989) has pointed out many ways in which under fives are already meeting expectations of children up to the age of seven. They encourage practitioners to continue to work in a way that puts children rather than curriculum content at the centre of their planning and recording. The group has also published a guide to show how the requirements of the revised programmes of study in the National Curriculum can be underpinned through a developmentally appropriate approach for children from five to seven (Early Years Curriculum Group, 1997).

Children at the centre of their learning

A learner-centred way of working provides an effective starting point for students of all ages, especially when they are in an unfamiliar setting. This is particularly true for young children, whose rate of development is very individual, and whose home surroundings give them very varied prior experience. In order for them to be able to show what they can do and to flourish as learners, under-fives need to feel secure in any new context and should have the support of adults who are able to pay sympathetic attention to their personal circumstances. This is why staffing ratios and relevant qualifications are so important. David, Curtis and Siraj-Blatchford (1993) draw attention to the key characteristics of the relationship between teaching and learning in the early years.

Adults asking questions

Margaret Donaldson (1978) explains how young children can demonstrate sophisticated levels of comprehension when they have an understanding of the context of complex questions. She underlines the idea that adults should 'decentre' and ensure that they consider children's points of view in framing learning experiences. Often children themselves give clear indications of the lack of logic of some of our assumptions and strategies: Sonnyboy, a traveller child of five who had not yet learned that one of the first rules of being a pupil is to be quiet and listen, inquired of his teacher: 'Why do you keep asking the kids questions when you knows all the answers? Like... like... what colour is it then? You can see for yourself it's red... so why do you keep asking them?' (Cousins, 1990, p.30).

As Katz points out (Katz and Chard, 1989), one effect of the excessive use of interrogations is to create phoney patterns of interaction, which may make respondents feel threatened. There is now a wealth of convincing evidence about the educational value of authentic discussions, where children and adults share a genuine interest, rather than sterile questioning to check whether children can provide answers that adults already know (Tizard and Hughes, 1984; Wells, 1987; Wood, 1988).

Developing language

The acquisition of language is a good example of the intellectual power of young children. It also highlights the fact that most adults are instinctively able to provide appropriate support for children's linguistic development, and to extend their experience and skills in a way that is closely matched to progress. This is a useful model for later teaching:

in addition to research on early literacy, influenced by Vygotsky's (1962) work on language development, there has been recent discussion on the value of a similar 'apprenticeship' approach to other forms of representation, with the adults providing a structure to match children's emerging skills.

(Gura, 1992; Matthews, 1995,
Gopnik, Meltzoff and Kuhn 1999)

Culture and expectations

Cultural differences may be misunderstood by adults who are not aware of what they themselves do not know. For example, the common view that four-year-olds should be able to use a knife and fork competently ignores the previous experience of many children who may have learned the skilful use of chopsticks or of their fingers rather than cutlery for eating at home. Although staff may not be able to familiarise themselves with every detail of children's personal frames of reference, it is certainly possible for them to share their appreciation of the varied patterns of behaviour that exist even within an indigenous group. Given a sympathetic lead, children are very quick to pick up on the ethos modelled by adults, and are well able to accept and begin to understand different expectations. Several of Vivien Gussin Paley's books vividly describe this process unfolding in her kindergarten class, expressed and explored through the children's ability to express their growing awareness through narrative (Paley, 1984, 1986, 1988, 1990).

Approaches to teaching and learning

What works for children?

Worries expressed by a government minister that an informal approach which takes into account children's individual interests will result in 'lots of fun and painting' but little serious learning are set to rest by findings from a recent project that considered attainment at the end of Key Stage 1, when children are six or seven. In 1994 the National Foundation for Educational Research undertook a multivariate analysis which showed that early entry to primary school for summer-born children did not result in higher achievement two or three years later (Sharp, Hutchison and Whetton, 1994; Sharp, 1995). Four-year-olds who remained in a nursery setting generally achieved better than a comparable group whose choices of both content and context were arbitrarily constrained in more formal infant classes. This is even more significant when taken together with findings that show how children may be turned off school by an instructional approach that does not take into account their past experience, their particular learning styles or their individual interests (Barrett, 1986).

Further evidence of the importance of what Dweck calls mastery (as opposed to performance) goals is quoted by Sylva (1994) and is supported by findings in her research on differences between children entering reception class after playgroup or nursery school experience (Jowett and Sylva, 1986). It appears that children who are given choices and genuine opportunities to take responsibility for their actions are more likely to use adults as a resource for learning instead of relying on them for approval, and to persevere in tackling difficulties rather than give up in the face of challenge. In order to sustain the confidence to ask questions, and to learn from mistakes, children must know that their voices will be heard and their individual needs and abilities observed and respected. This is clearly expressed as a right in articles 12 and 13 of the UN Convention on the Rights of the Child and is also consistent with the traditional approach to nursery education in the UK. It has been well expressed by HMI in their commentary on the education of under-fives (DES, 1989) and in the Rumbold Report (DES, 1990). Many locally developed documents that guide practice across services in different parts of England also recommend a child-centred pedagogy and counsel against too formal an approach too soon (see, for example, Westminster Education Authority, 1992; Hampshire Education Authority, 1995; Newham Education Authority, 1995).

Early childhood specialists have been promoting the value of a non-directive way of working for many years. Part of the skill of the educator is to enable a harmonious flow of activity to continue, which depends on children being able to take considerable responsibility for their own needs. Adults are thus free to work with individuals or small groups on planned or spontaneous topics. The more skilfully this is done, the easier it looks to an outside observer. It does, however, require significant forethought and organisation based on professional knowledge of child development and of the individual characteristics of any particular group of children. There is increasing evidence to show that this kind of interactive approach, recommended and put into practice by Susan Isaacs in the 1930s and the McMillan sisters before that, is effective because it allows for physical, emotional and social growth alongside intellectual development. Recent work on the importance of the social dimension of learning (Trevarthen, 1992b) and of the long-term effects of affective dispositions to learn (Katz and McLellan, 1991; Roberts, 1995) help to explain ways of working that have already proved themselves empirically.

Developing curriculum

'Quality in Diversity', an initiative undertaken by the multi-agency Early Childhood Education Forum across the UK, has drawn up a framework for the early years curriculum, with the following headings:

- Being and Becoming
- Belonging and Connecting
- Participating and Contributing
- Thinking
- Doing
- Being Active

These headings underline the integrated nature of learning in the early years, and have been devised to provide a useful framework which can be interpreted by people working with young children in different settings. Each staff group will have the responsibility of providing their own structure and activities to express in practice the principles set out in the framework. This multi-professional undertaking in the UK has been influenced by recent work in New Zealand (Ministry of Education, 1993) which envisages the early childhood curriculum as a 'whariki', or mat, woven from the principles, aims, and goals defined in the Ministry of Education guidelines. Different programmes, philosophies, structures and environments contribute to the distinctive patterns of the varied interpretations of the 'Te Whariki' framework. This approach to the curriculum is designed to promote children's rights, and fits well with the principles and articles of the UN Convention. Every educator could examine his or her view of education and the curriculum he or she plans for children in the light of the headings developed by the UK Quality in Diversity project, to see how his or her work links to them.

When children in one of the pre-schools in the Emilia Romagna region of Italy were invited to describe what they saw as their own rights, one girl commented. 'Children have the right to think their thoughts, because it's them that have to think about what they want to do' (Reggio Children, 1995), and a boy stated that 'Freedom is the right to know things' (ibid).

The fact that children around five years of age are able to express themselves so thoughtfully demonstrates the profound capabilities children can develop when their views and ideas are respected and when adults find appropriate ways to work with them. Loris Malaguzzi, who did so much to articulate the philosophy behind the work with young children and the community in Reggio Emilia, has expressed the underlying principles as follows:

Children have the right to be active participants in the organisation of their identities, abilities and autonomy, through relationships and interaction with their peers, with adults, ideas, things, and with the real and imaginary events of intercommunicating worlds. All this... also credits children, and each individual child, with inborn abilities and potential that are extraordinarily rich, powerful and creative... this is so much truer when children are reassured by an effective alliance between the adults in their lives, adults who... place more importance on the search for constructive strategies of thought and action than on the direct transmission of knowledge and skills.

(Malaguzzi, 1992)

Environments for learning

Bruce (1987) confirms that children need time and scope to develop their own ideas, to explore and investigate new possibilities alongside sympathetic adults, and to engage in self-regulated practice. In order to enable this to happen, planning and organisation within early years settings need to be structured to cover the wide range of learning opportunities that will lead to the early learning goals to be introduced for children at the end of the reception year (QCA 2000).

In addition to providing scope for language and mathematical development, staff should enable children to find out about the world through activities that stimulate scientific and technological exploration. An awareness of their own environment and past and present events in their own lives is the starting point for children's learning about geography and history. If they are to meet these expectations when they reach five or six, under fives need plenty of scope to investigate their world actively, and to express themselves creatively in a wide variety of ways.

As part of planning for all these areas of experience, and ensuring that children's physical, social and emotional development flourishes alongside their intellectual growth, staff must allow for unexpected as well as planned opportunities for learning to be followed up appropriately, assessed and recorded, and shared with parents and carers. It is useful if resources, both indoors and out, can be stored so that children can select and reach them independently, and use them to meet their intended purposes. A wide range of tools and equipment is needed to support children's learning across the curriculum, and the way that they are kept can in itself stimulate learning: for example, recycled materials such as empty cereal packets and other containers can be organised according to size and shape, so that they may reinforce mathematical thinking as well as contribute to children's physical and technological development as they construct 3D representations of their ideas. It should be possible to promote the refinement and extension of these ideas by providing a place to keep ongoing work, and by encouraging children to discuss their strategies. Children can contribute constructive comments on one another's work, and in the process become more discriminating and articulate: it is very desirable that group work should include the opportunity for more experienced learners to pass on techniques and information, as well as being the recipients of instructions themselves. Younger or less experienced children are well able to follow a lead and participate in activities which they cannot yet initiate (Katz and Chard, 1989).

The role of the adult goes beyond collecting, selecting, arranging and maintaining the environment and facilitating work and play in varied groups. Evaluative, reciprocal discussion with children can encourage more accurate representations; scribing children's comments and incorporating these in a display of work reinforces both the worth of what they say and the value of literacy development. It also makes a significant contribution towards what Vygotsky (Bruner, Jolly and Sylva, 1976) called second order representation, an essential tool for later more abstract learning.

Adults should hold back from telling children directly how to solve their problems: it is in choosing, experimenting and finding ways of correcting any 'mistakes' that children make learning their own, both in terms of intellectual awareness and in developing the dispositions to be selective, weigh evidence and persevere in the face of difficulties. We in England are at last able to re-claim territory lost over years of top-down prescription for teaching to set outcomes, because play is now officially recognised as a crucial medium for learning in the early years. There is also a welcome new emphasis on communication and creativity. This could well extend beyond the bounds of school or nursery, and influence relationships between practitioners, parents and the wider community. In this way, we can foster the development of a mutually respectful learning society, in line with the aspirations of the United Nations Convention on the Rights of the Child.

Contact:

Wendy Scott, Chief Executive,
The British Association of Early Childhood Education,
136 Cavell Street, London, E1 2JA

References

This article is an edited version of *Choices in Learning,* in *Respectful Educations, Capable Learners – Children's Rights and Early Education,* edited by Cathy Nutbrown, published by Paul Chapman, London, 1996.

See the latter book for detailed references.

3. Starting with Children – Towards an Early Years Curriculum

Mary Jane Drummond

The Japanese have a word for it – *kodomorashii kodomo,* translated by Tobin, Wu and Davidson (1976) as 'a child-like child.' Their fascinating cross-cultural study, *Preschool in Three Cultures,* introduces the concept of the child-like child in the context of a lively debate between early years educators from Japan, China and the USA. The debate is stimulated by video-tape presentations of a typical day in a kindergarten in each of the 'three cultures', and its liveliness stems from the startling differences in approach revealed by the videos. There are differences to be discussed in almost every aspect of daily practice; the Chinese group trips to the toilet, for example, make very disturbing viewing for the US and Japanese educators.

But the more important differences run deeper than this: differences of principle and purpose, philosophy and mission. The notion of the child-like child, so familiar to the Japanese educators, so challenging to the other parties to the debate, suggests how deep these differences can be. What is at stake is the way in which educators of whatever nation choose to think about the children for whose early years they have taken responsibility. In answering the question – 'What *is* a child-like child, in our society?' educators and others (parents, politicians, philosophers) are forced to explore deeply held but rarely examined values and principles, in order to establish the basis for their curriculum and pedagogy.

Such an exploration is long overdue in this country. As we set about the process of reviewing and renewing a curriculum framework to take us into the millennium, I believe we will do well to start by finding our own answers to the fundamental question that runs through every page of *Preschool in Three Cultures*. What *do* we want for our young, child-like children? If we can answer this question, it seems to me we will be in a good position to work on constructing a curriculum fit for young children.

In the process of examining our own values and beliefs however, we would be foolish to neglect the work of other educators, past and present, near at hand and far away, who have much to teach us about young children and their learning. A critical and respectful scrutiny of the work of others will be an essential part of our own enterprise. For example, we might begin in Italy, in the prosperous region of Emilia-Romagna, where services to young children, from birth to three, and from three to six, are rightly world-famous. Their travelling exhibit *The 100 Languages of Children* is just coming to the end of its second visit to the UK (the first was in 1997). The title of this exhibition is a reference to the principle at the heart of their approach, which is recognition of children's powers as communicators. The Italian educators starkly represent this central idea with a slogan: 'Children speak 100 languages, 99 of which are ignored in school.' They try to do better in their pre-schools and day-care centres and nurseries, every one of which is furnished with an *atelier,* a workshop staffed by an *atelierista,* a trained professional artist and educator. In the *atelier,* children's capacities for representing the world around them, and expressing their responses to, and relationships with that world are, from the earliest age, fostered and extended (Edwards et al 1993).

For the Italians, children's acts of representation and expression are the foundations for all subsequent learning. So, for example, their approach to literacy starts from the concept of exchange- 'lo scambio'; not with the book, or the story, or the printed word, but with the early capacity of the baby and the toddler to communicate in a give-and-take process of exchange. The exchange of a look, a smile, a touch, between the baby and the primary care-givers is, for the Italian educators, the beginning of all one hundred of children's symbolic languages, including the language of books and the world of print. Their earliest provision for this foundation stone of learning is again, not the book, as it is here, but a structure of tiny pigeon holes, one for each child and adult educator, labelled with names and photographs, for the exchange of meaningful messages between children and adults. The youngest children post each other stones, flowers, biscuits, fetishes and tiny treasures; the older ones exchange marks, drawings, letters, notes and news bulletins. These children are not only learning to read and write, they are learning to give and to receive. Carla Rinaldi, a pedagogical co-ordinator who works to support curriculum development in a group of pre-schools and nurseries, summarises their approach:

The cornerstone of our experience, based on practice, theory and research, is the image of children as rich, strong and powerful... They have... the desire to grow, curiosity, the ability to be amazed and the desire to relate to other people and to communicate... Children are eager to express themselves within the context of a plurality of symbolic languages... Children are open to exchanges and reciprocity as deeds and acts of love which they not only want to receive but also want to offer.

(Edwards et al 1993 p. 102-3)

In describing the Reggio-Emilia approach I am not advocating slavish imitation, or suggesting that we swallow someone else's programme whole. But I am convinced that we can learn from other educators, and the possibilities that their work suggests. In particular we can learn from approaches where children, and their learning, are the starting points for the educators' thinking. The New Zealand early years curriculum framework *Te Whariki* (Ministry of Education 1996) is one such approach. The Maori words of the title refer to traditional woven mats, with an infinite variety of patterns; the guidelines envisage the early childhood curriculum as such a mat, woven from the principles, aims and goals defined in the document. The Whariki concept represents, in a vivid and meaningful way, the diversity of early childhood education in New Zealand: from common starting points, each provision creates its own distinctive pattern. The five aims, on which the whole framework is based, are:

- Well-being: the health and well-being of the child is protected and nurtured;
- Belonging: children and their families feel a sense of belonging;
- Contribution: opportunities for learning are equitable, and each child's contribution is valued;
- Communication: the languages and symbols of children's own and other cultures are promoted and protected;
- Exploration: the child learns through active exploration of the environment.

I have argued elsewhere that the New Zealand document is especially challenging for educators in the UK because of the values at its core (Drummond 1996). Our own National Curriculum, we ruefully remember as we read *Te Whariki,* is constructed around Maths, English and Science, rather than belonging and contributing. Our current approach is prescriptive, rather than principled; and so, as we set about reaffirming our principles and purposes in early years education, we cannot afford to ignore the way in which the New Zealand educators make their case.

In this country too, there have been educators who still have much to teach us about children's learning. The great progressive (and one-time chief inspector of schools) Edmond Holmes summarises his life's work in a vision of children's learning as growth – growth towards truth (stemming from the desire to enquire, to know and understand), towards beauty (from the desire to express oneself and to delight in the creative arts) and towards love (from the desire to communicate, to imagine, to identify one's life with others.) (Holmes 1911).

Across the channel in Belgium, Ovide Decroly (born in 1871) built an early years curriculum around the principle of active learning. His schools, which flourished in the first quarter of this century, were organised around the child's experiences 'in close contact with the real, the actual.' 'Let the child prepare for life by living' was his slogan, and the detailed curriculum plans that survive in a contemporary account demonstrate Decroly's commitment to the processes, rather than the products of early learning: 'To perceive – to think – to act, and to express – we must not lose sight of that sequence.' (Hamaide 1925) This brief summary does not, or course, do justice to Decroly's conceptualisation of teaching and learning, and yet, in a way, the essence of his work is conveyed by the power of those four active verbs – to perceive, to think, to act, and to express. An even tighter formulation can be found in the work of Diderot and the group of radical philosophers who together created the great Encyclopaedia, published in 35 volumes between 1751 and 1776. In these volumes the whole of human understanding is subsumed under just three heads: Memory, Reason and

Imagination (Furbank 1992). Again, I am not making a case for nostalgia: I am proposing that we use the richness of our collective educational past and present to help us envisage and grasp the future.

As our debate proceeds, informed, let us hope, by an eclectic richness of reference, we will need guiding principles to support us in making choices. The first of these, I suggest, should be that we concentrate on children's strengths rather than their weaknesses, their capabilities rather than their incapacities, on their considerable intellectual and emotional powers, as we know them from generations of research and enquiry. My own sense of children's powers has developed both from my reading of psychology and philosophy, and from my observations, over the years, of young children living and learning in a whole variety of settings. Children's powers, their powers to do, to feel, to think, to know and understand, to represent and express, constitute for me the most appropriate starting point for thinking about an early years curriculum. By starting here, we will be able to construct a curriculum that does justice to these powers, that strengthens and develops them, throughout the first six or seven years of their life. In the process we will be able to continue the debate: what kinds of thinking, doing and feeling do we aspire to for our child-like children?

As we extend and elaborate our lists of children's powers, adding the active verbs that we value most dearly (for example, the power to ask questions, to imagine, to speak more than one language, to sorrow, to wonder, to console) we will be making progress in our enterprise. The next step is to see how such a list, however short or long, can be transformed into children's lived experiences. Here my thinking is supported by the unjustly neglected writer George MacDonald, once famous for his children's stories *(The Princess and the Goblin, At the Back of the North Wind)*. Writing of the central importance of the imagination in children's spiritual and moral development, MacDonald advises us how to proceed:

If we speak of direct means for the culture of the imagination, the whole is comprised in two words – food and exercise...

(MacDonald 1882 p. 36)

I propose that we kidnap these categories, and hold them up against our consideration of children's powers, asking ourselves what food and what exercise will sustain and strengthen our child-like children.

The 'food' we set before our young children is, as it were, the stuff of curriculum: the stuff in the cupboards, the photocopier, the garden, the clay bin and the *atelier* (see also Anne Fine's *The Granny Project* for a brilliant analysis of the Social Science curriculum as *stuff*). But stuff is not enough; children also need daily opportunities to exercise their growing powers, their intellectual and emotional muscles. In their scientific studies, for example, young children will encounter, amongst other things, woodlice, gravity, shadows, seaweed, moss, yeast and water; but these first-hand experiences are not enough. They must also act as scientists, observing, comparing, connecting and demanding explanations. There must be time and space and opportunities for them to exercise these developing powers, to flex their growing muscles. The more opportunities there are, the more exercise they will take. As R. A. Hodgkin so memorably puts it,

Rather than asking, 'what stick or carrot will make children active in certain ways; or what will make them go in this direction rather than that?', we would do well to turn the problem round and to say: children will go in any case, for it is an expression of their being to be purposeful and energetic...

(Hodgkin 1985)

Conclusion

In recent years, discussion about the National Curriculum and the new curriculum for teacher training has been dominated by the subject-specialists, and the core and foundation subjects established by the 1988 Education Reform Act.

I have argued here that in developing an early years curriculum we would do better to *start with children,* taking into account everything we know about their learning, their motivation, and their impressive intellectual and emotional powers. In so doing, we will be able to express and implement our most dearly held aspirations for the education of the child-like children of the future.

Mary Jane Drummond is a lecturer at the School of Education, University of Cambridge. She started teaching in an overcrowded infant school in London's East End in 1966 and since then has taught in a variety of inner city primary schools; she was the headteacher of a school in Sheffield for four years.

In 1985 she joined the Institute of Education in Cambridge, an in-service institution working for teachers and other educators all over East Anglia, which was incorporated into the University of Cambridge in 1992. Her work has become increasingly interdisciplinary, and her Early Years courses are now attended by educators from the education and social services, and from the voluntary sector. She has close links with the Early Childhood Unit at the National Children's Bureau, and with them has published two in-service development packs of materials for early years educators. Her book, *Assessing Children's Learning* (1993) is published by David Fulton in the UK, and by Stenhouse in the US and Canada.

Contact:

School of Education, University of Cambridge
Shaftesbury Road, Cambridge CB2 2BX

Tel: (01223) 369631
Fax: (01223) 324421
E-mail: sf207@cam.ac.uk

References

Drummond, M. J. (1996) 'Play, Learning and the National Curriculum – some possibilities' in Cox, T. (ed.) *The National Curriculum and the Early Years.* London: The Falmer Press.

Edwards, C., Gandini, L. & Forman, G. (eds.) (1993). *The Hundred Languages of Children: The Reggio Emilia Approach to Early Childhood Education.* Norwood, New Jersey: Ablex Publishing Corporation.

Fine, A. (1990) *The Granny Project.* London: Mammoth.

Furbank, P. N. (1992) *Diderot, A Critical Biography.* London: Minerva.

Hamaide, A. (1925) *The Decroly Class: A Contribution to Elementary Education.* London: J. M. Dent.

Holmes, E. (1911) *What Is and What Might Be.* London: Constable.

Hodgkin, R. A. (1985) *Playing & Exploring.* London: Methuen.

MacDonald, G. (1882) *Orts.* London: Sampson Low, Marston, Searle, & Rivington.

Ministry of Education, New Zealand (1996) *Te Whariki. Early Childhood Curriculum.* Wellington, New Zealand: Learning Media.

Tobin, J. J., Wu, D., Davidson, D. (1989) *Preschool in Three Cultures.* New Haven: Yale University Press.

This chapter is reproduced, with permission, from *Take Care, Mr. Blunkett: powerful voices in the new curriculum debate* published in 1998 by the Association of Teachers and Lecturers.

4. Childhood Matters: the present future – A Steiner Waldorf perspective

Sally Jenkinson

In her book *Children's Minds*, Margaret Donaldson includes a memorable extract from *Cider With Rosie* in which a young and somewhat disgruntled Laurie Lee tells his family about his first day at school. 'You just sit there **for the present**' he had apparently been told. He complains bitterly that though he sat and waited all day long, the anticipated present completely failed to materialise. 'I never got it. I ain't going back there again,' he says.

This little vignette exposes the child's misunderstanding, his 'ambiguity where we would see none' (Donaldson p 17) and his subsequent disappointment with the experience of school, which to his young mind promised much but failed to deliver.

The charge that school had never given him the present has another layer of meaning. Across the span of life, it is as children that we are most 'present'. Engrossed in the moment and lacking discrimination and the filter of cynicism, young children are healthily interested in everything: the distant stars vying equally for their attention with the enchanting, dirt-filled cracks of the pavement at their feet.

Yet despite their energetic determination to learn and explore at their own pace, children have always been drawn out of the fascinating and absorbing world of the present to attend to adult demands and needs, or to be trained (as opposed to educated) to serve future-oriented goals.

In fact, the practice of hurrying children out of childhood has a long and shameful past. Adults have always expected even very young children to work for them. In the 1900's one quarter of all London's children aged 5-13 were working in paid jobs outside school. Compulsory education had been introduced with the aim of removing children from the exploitative child labour market to the work of the schoolroom. 'Children were now required to do *school* work as opposed to waged labour… [and] for the majority, [it was] school work devised to produce an obedient and unquestioning labour force for the new factories and offices.' (Humphries, Mack, Perks 1998 p.27) Education was often brutal and authoritarian: exploitation dressed in the more acceptable guise of reform.

In contrast, guided by the principle of education towards freedom, the first 'Steiner' school was founded in 1919. Following a series of inspiring lectures given by Rudolf Steiner, the workers at the Waldorf cigarette factory in Stuttgart asked him for a school for their children. Steiner's aim was to create an education that would value and respect each person's right to their own thoughts, feelings and actions, whatever their background or circumstances, which would attend to the child's needs before those of the nation. Children would not be hurried out of childhood to serve extrinsic future needs. It was the child's present needs which would take precedence.

Some twenty years after Rudolf Steiner's death the Nazis closed down this school – and six sister schools. They argued that Germany had no room for two kinds of education – one that educated citizens for the state and another that taught children to think for themselves. (Oppenheimer Atlantic Monthly 1999)

Rudolf Steiner's deepest wish was to equip young people with the kind of qualities: clarity of thought, sensitivity of feeling, and purposeful will needed to generate a new social order and a new sense of ethics. Qualities that amongst other things would generate alternatives to war as a means of resolving conflict.

He said: 'We should not ask: what does a person need to know or be able to do in order to fit into the existing social order? Instead we should ask: what lives in every human being and what can be developed in him or her? Only then will it be possible to direct the new qualities of each emerging generation into society. Society will then become what young people as whole human beings make out of the existing social conditions. The new generation should not just be made to be what present society wants it to become!' (Steiner Waldorf Schools Fellowship leaflet 1999)

This is the abiding motif behind the Steiner-teacher's approach to the child: what lives in you now and what will develop in you over time? Implicit in this attitude is a willingness to notice, and work with what presents itself (a present again) in the individual at different stages; a freedom from external imposition and a profound respect for the unfolding processes of time. Living today *fully* sets the arrow of the future on its true course.

The Unhurried Journey and the Morality of Time

Today's children, like Laurie Lee, are not being *given the present* in many other ways. A survey carried out in the United States found that the most common phrase addressed to children in the morning was 'Hurry Up!' A revealing and salutary commentary on adult attitudes to children and childhood and to the very different time frames within which children and adults operate.

Jay Griffiths, author of 'The Morality of Time', argues that all ideas about time have a moral component. Our society, he claims, is hooked on speed and has made the pleasure of encounter, the joy of the long lingering moment and the wisdom of reflection subservient to the virtue of speed. Formerly, societies looked backwards for the wisdom of their ancestors, or forwards with a duty of care towards their descendants. Today, he claims, we are 'Disrespectful of the past and careless of humanity's future.'

Ultimately, the fate of the earth itself lies in our ability to understand time: to grasp the critical relationship between exploitation and regeneration. Greed and speed equal depletion of energy. Technological time has usurped natural time and made slaves of us all.

In real time, writes Griffiths, 'Children live with Alice in a slowed up Wonderland, and they, like Alice, find the fussing, hurrying, speeding, watch-ridden white Rabbit very very silly indeed. I have met the White Rabbit… He is a dealer in foreign exchange… hyperalert, [he] speaks terribly quickly, his eyes are bloodshot and darting all over the place, his breath is jerky. He says he is addicted to adrenaline and works in hypermode and admits if you don't enjoy the rushes, you can't do the job. He is a man in love with speed. He describes his faults as speed-related; being easily frustrated by people, short-tempered and intolerant. His personal calls last, on average, five seconds. I asked him if his friends were intimidated at the speed he was going at? Maybe, he said, yes, but half the time I don't notice. I'm going too fast.' (Griffiths 1999 p.3)

The intensity of our fast-forward focus on the future and on acquisition and competition affects our attitudes to the most vulnerable group in our society. Our children are responding with a range of 'time-deprivation behaviours'. Their voices are speaking to us – if only we can take the time to listen. An interesting new phenomenon recently highlighted in the press illustrates this point. In certain households as soon as the children get home from school they put on their pyjamas, and on

Saturdays they wear them for as long as possible – all day if they can. This strategy prevents their parents from taking them out to yet another *'don't be ungrateful it's for your own good'* – maths, piano, ballet, gym, tennis lesson. The children's behaviour makes it clear that all they want to do is to simply mess around, be themselves for a while, and live in their own time; hence the 'pyjama defence.' Every evening and weekend hoards of small and weary trophy hunters are ferried about in cars to bring back the spoils for their eager parents. We parents are victims too. In the grip of the speed neurosis ourselves, we have forgotten to notice that our children excel in **being,** as Eric Fromm perceptively observed in his book 'To Have or to Be' (Fromm 1997). The 'needing to have' state leads to dissatisfaction with the 'what is.'

Libby Purves expresses concern about the human cost incurred in this drive for acceleration, observing that,

...given sand, water, and a bucket an infant will unaidedly do physics, maths, resistant materials technology, design, hydraulics and (if burbling) language. A child burying an offending teddy head-first in the sand is doing ethics and drama; up-ending a bucket of water on his head is a fine training in comedy which may lead to a Bafta.

What is served by interfering with this personal curriculum because it is time to chant ABC or colour in tedious worksheets? Adult convenience is served, certainly: and parental neurosis about education, and government statistics fed by measurable results. But you've wrecked the game and impoverished the child.

(Purves 15/06/99 Times)

Inevitably, this insidious and unnecessary impoverishment – poverty of the imagination and poverty of choice – has the most severe impact upon those children already short-changed by their life circumstances.

Convenience Childhood?

Evidence from the USA suggests that powerful psychotropic drugs are routinely administered to children as young as two – without diagnosis and in the absence of medical symptoms – in order to control their behaviour. Placed in inappropriately formal day care nurseries, to fit in with the long hours of adult work schedules, two-year-olds are dosed with modifying drugs to 'treat' their quite normal, but inconvenient, age-appropriate behaviours. Under pressure to conform to standards of behaviour previously expected from school children they are medicated and sedated.

Powerful drugs are also prescribed for ADHD-diagnosed children who show a disturbed relationship to time. In this painfully speeded-up world of ours, time intensive help based on emotional contact, commitment, patience, love and trust, is being superseded by the quick chemical fix which desensitises the child and effectively masks the symptoms of his/her individual problem/need. Children are regulated and controlled by chemical time dispensing with the need for time-consuming interventions and therapy.

In the UK one in 5 children, between the ages of 4 and 20, show signs of stress – another symptom of time disorder. Pressures to 'keep up' begin almost at birth. The human *race* is aptly named. (Bright Futures: The Big Picture, interim report published by the Mental Health Foundation 1999)

Speed obviously has advantages. Mowing the lawn with my Flymo takes less than half the time than if I had used the back-breakingly heavy mower my mother once pushed, and it leaves me with more energy for other things, But, and this is a big but, need we use speed so indiscriminately? Why should speed be an advantage when applied to education, for example? When given the opportunity, young children, along with poets, artists and scientists, live in slowed-up time: they notice things. They spend hours looking into the vast and tiny gallery of world exhibits newly displayed each day. In child time, slowed-up time, (even as an adult), one may see the world afresh, with heightened senses. This is the true gift of the present. Why rush to the future?

The *Bright Future Report* concludes with these words:

A truly child-nurturing society would be one where children were fully integrated rather than separated and where their needs were understood and were regarded as at least of equal importance as those of adults... We seem to have lost sight of what it feels like to be a child and of the connection between the child and the adult self.

In out of school hours fear of the outdoor environment as a safe place to play has meant a move from freely chosen, involved, social, activities to static, asocial, sensory-deficient passive TV watching. First-hand *experience* is passed-over in favour of second hand *entertainment* – benefiting TV companies and commercial markets but once again 'impoverishing the child.'

Children have become increasingly alienated from real life and from each other. Diverted from their own tasks by the advert-laden, consumerist values of commercialism, the silent, passive watchers grow distant. Life is on pause for them. Chemical time and technological time replace child-time, human time.

When adults watch TV, according to Marie Winn, author of *The Plug-In Drug,* they refer to 'a vast backlog of real life experiences.' 'As the adult watches television, she argues, 'his own present and past relationships, experiences, dreams, and fantasies come into play, transforming the material he sees, whatever its origins or purpose, into something reflecting his own particular needs.' Children, she explains, do not have this background of real life experience and for many of them, TV watching constitutes a *primary* activity. Programmes are referenced by other programmes rather than by real life experiences. 'Children's early television experiences, she believes will, to some extent, '…serve to de-humanize, to mechanize, to make less *real* the realities and relation-ships they encounter in life. For them, real events will always carry subtle echoes of the television world.' (Winn p.10, 11)

In the USA pre-schoolers are the single largest TV audience, watching some 54 hours per week. These, and other similarly alarming statistics, prompted a group of Americans to launch a 'National Turn off TV week'. A list of 100 things to do instead of watching television was made available to anyone calling a given number. The response was amazing: the lines were jammed for days. The list included suggestions such as: 'Watch a sunset together' or 'Bake some cookies' – simple communal pleasures, rooted in real time. It wasn't only the children who benefited from this campaign, as the many expressions of thanks from adults who had rediscovered forgotten pleasures demonstrated.

Children suffer physically from the long-term consequences of TV-induced immobility. When not watching, they are naturally fidgety, admirably inquisitive and irrepressibly active – unless physical circumstances determine otherwise. Even in moments of deep concentration and apparent stillness, it is the active involvement in the chosen task which keeps the child engaged. In optimum conditions, being made to sit still is a form of torment, as those who use it as a means of control and punishment unfortunately know too well. TV watching achieves total control effortlessly, which is why it is such an efficient child-minder. Only illness, sleep and a depressed sense of well-being induce comparable periods of prolonged stillness. A diminution of consciousness is the common factor in all these states of being. (TV watching produces similar brain-waves to those observed in sleep).

Extensive watching effectively freezes the wonderfully imaginative movement tutorial, which playful children design for themselves at all stages of their development. Through movement, new skills are gained as increasing motor control gradually brings co-ordination and bodily grace. A good day's play makes a child feel healthy, physically at rest and at home in his body. Conversely, after heavy TV watching, a compensatory period of disordered, hyperactive movement usually occurs. Many of today's children go to bed with over-stimulated nervous systems and under-exercised bodies, resulting in disturbed sleep patterns which, in a horribly circular way, are then controlled by drugs.

Dr. Peter Struck, expressing concern about the physical effects of 'parking' children in front of the TV, writes:

...children who have too seldom run and jumped, who have had insufficient opportunity to play on a swing or in the mud, to climb and to balance, will have difficulty walking backwards. They lag behind in arithmetic and appear to be clumsy and stiff. These children cannot accurately judge strength, speed, or distance; and thus they are more accident prone than other children.

[In Germany] ...two thirds of all school children listen to music droning from gigantic boom boxes, Walkmen and Diskmen. Among elementary school age children, one in three already possesses his or her own television and one in five his or her own computer.

...one in ten adolescents already suffers hearing loss; 60% of children entering school have poor posture, 35% are overweight, 40% have poor circulation. 38% cannot adequately co-ordinate their arms and legs, and more than 50% lack stamina for running, jumping and swimming.

(Struck 1999 p. 31)

Advertising agencies are openly engaged in a full-scale assault upon childhood. Through impossibly attractive images they appeal to children's vulnerabilities and those of their parents. Relying on 'pester power', children are exploited into persuading or haranguing their parents to make purchases. The crying child in the supermarket who wants what he has seen on TV is a sadly familiar figure. Shopping trips become a nightmare for parents.

The delightfully idiosyncratic and unpredictable fads of childhood are now deliberately stage-managed for profit. Every new film or computer generates profitable product lines – the 'must-have' toys.

The strategic campaign to advertise and sell Pokémon cards is a case in point. After high TV profiling, certain cards were deliberately limited to increase desirability and rarity value. This led to bullying and acts of desperation amongst children. A seven-year old offered to swap his first newly pulled baby tooth, presumably because of its under-the-pillow value; his gap-less friends refused it, sensing credibility problems at home perhaps. But what else had he to offer? Another boy went so far as to offer his sister in exchange for the desired card… Why do we reduce children to this helpless and humiliating state? Enhanced or reduced status and self-esteem are measured by possession, or the lack of, the right products: market forces rule the playground. Manipulative advertisers understand this painful social dynamic and employ it in a abuse of power. Our children, who rightly own nothing and thus everything, are cynically reduced and degraded by their own exploited feelings.

Away from the compulsions and obsessions engendered by the TV, video and computer, children are busy learning to belong, and to value others in ways which don't require acquisition or ownership. In the opinion of Vivian Gussin Paley, author of the inspiringly titled book, *The Kindness of Children,* they learn in ways which build a social and ethical world.

If the need to know how someone else feels is the rock upon which the moral universe depends, then the ancient sages were right. For this is surely what happens when children give each other roles to play in their continual inquiry into the nature of human connections. It is as schoolchildren that we begin life's investigations of those weighty matters.

(Paley, 1999, p.61)

Paley quotes a colleague: 'And what do the children philosophise about? How to gain access to every person, feeling, thing and event.' (Paley, 1999, p.67). Children want to understand life, to feel the fabric of society and to access their culture. They want to work out what makes people and things tick. Their way of doing this is through play.

I witnessed and became involved in cultural access play in a shopping game, which some children were playing in a kindergarten in York. Both real and pretend shopping requires specific cultural knowledge and playing shops authentically involves many skills. When I asked if I could buy something, I was told irritably that I would need money *of course*. Of course, but where was money exactly? Money was in the *bank, 'over there'*, said the harassed shop assistant gesturing with a sweep of her arm, towards some shelves behind me. Returning, I offered my conkers, which I had (wrongly) assumed to be money. *'That's not money'*, she said with disdain, *'shells are, of course.'* Of course. After another trip to the bank and now finally equipped with the right currency – some small shells and a large flat one, I returned for another try. 'I'd like some potatoes please,' I said. Grudgingly, my potatoes (these were conkers) were put into a little bag. Then came a surprise. The bag was held at waist level, and then moved across the worksurface with slow deliberation. As it was held and moved in this formalised way, a perfectly synchronised 'beep' accompanied the mid-point of the transaction. My purchase had been scanned! I had hardly registered my amazement when I was asked to hand over my credit card: the flat shell. This was expertly swiped through an invisible machine and I was asked, with the hint of a friendly smile, to sign the payment slip.

The game continued as I moved on and I noticed the queue growing. I was inspired by the girl's mastery of the situation. The level of knowledge based on her own, free observations and intuitions, which she was able to bring to her play-creation, was remarkable. She was, scripting, acting, directing and performing the play as it was happening. The serious business of modern shopping had been faithfully re-created down to the smallest detail. Those small eyes and ears waiting at the check-out counter in the real shop had missed nothing. Here were children finding ways to access their culture and to master it. By using representation and imagination, they were living into the rules and rituals of purchase without needing to buy a thing. They were finding out how others might feel and think and act. Though they owned nothing at the end of the game, their richness of understanding and ability to act in the world had increased dramatically. So had mine. The contrast between the emotionally intense Pokémon 'games' and the symbolic shopping experience could not be greater.

The need for a play-based curriculum to offset over-exposure to the artificial time frames imposed by TV, computers, behaviour modifiers and accelerated learning programmes has never been greater. Children deserve a curriculum which allows them time to develop empathy, to form relationships; to watch how things are done, to join in, to imitate, to wonder about things, to learn how to belong and to be allowed to be a child without fear of ridicule or shame.

In a slowed-up wonderland free from the world of white rabbit scheduling, children might be given over once more to wondering at and about the world. Must we set the clock to tick through childhood at such a rapid pace? Do we dare to value 'horizontal enrichment' over 'vertical acceleration?' (Elkind 1997, p122)

Written in the language of an earlier time – which may seem sentimental to a modern reader, George Eliot, in *The Mill on the*

Floss, gives a sweet yet powerful description of a 'horizontally enriched' childhood.

Life did change for Tom and Maggie and yet they were not wrong in believing that the thoughts and loves of these first years would always make part of their lives. We could never have loved the earth so well if we had had no childhood in it... What novelty is worth that sweet monotony where everything is known and loved because it is known... Our delight in the sunshine on the deep bladed grass today, might be no more than the faint perception of wearied souls, if it were not for the sunshine and the grass in the far-off years, which still live in us and transform our perception into love.

(Eliot 1985, p94)

The threads of our childhood perceptions filter upwards and become integrated into our personalities. Our futures are built on our present perceptions, and the quality of our early encounters with the world, have the greatest, and most lasting influence over us. Deep knowledge, deep concentration, deep play bring deep satisfaction and contentment with life.

Can we imagine ourselves back into that place of discovery when the world was new, to that time when we were thrilled by our senses? Are we able to recapture the intense curiosity we had about the fascinating world we found ourselves in, and can we empathise with those in that state of being now?

Horizontal enrichment – sensory education

In the Waldorf Kindergarten, attention to the senses is an important part of 'horizontal enrichment.' Rudolf Steiner suggested that in addition to the five senses (sight, hearing, touch, taste, smell), there were seven others. These included: the sense of life (of one's own well-being), of movement, balance, warmth, the sense for sound, the sense for speech, the sense for the perception of the thoughts of others and the sense for grasping the ego of the other. The combined working together of all our senses gives us the ability to make informed judgements and to establish a rounded view on life, he said.

Current studies show that children, '…who do not have enough tactile experience have difficulty becoming accustomed to social and emotional intimacy. The senses used in physical intimacy (touch, muscular co-ordination and sense of balance) are weakened through the lack of sufficient stimulation.' (Struck p.31) Holding on to a picture of the sensory landscape can be a helpful framework for parents and other educators to work with. Have each of the child's senses been enlivened and thus educated by experience? Have I provided enough opportunities for sensory encounters to happen?

Through healthy use of their senses, children first practise dialectics in the oppositions between things: hot, cold, dry, wet (notes from Glöckler, Dornach 1999). They learn subtlety and gradation and begin to build a personal feeling life: a sensory memory. They also enjoy themselves! A richly orchestrated sense life through feeling becomes the basis of a complex differentiated life of thought and the life of the fingers prepares the life of the mind!

There's no time like the present

In the Steiner kindergarten, time is slowed-up but not down. There is continuity, safety and security. Adults have time to be focused on the now. Time to be available for the child: to meet her needs when they arise. There is time to make something: a wooden spoon, a new doll or a carved boat, perhaps. Creative processes, which the children can follow, from start to finish, require a substantial time-commitment and a degree of skill from the adult. Careful, transparent, accessible adult work imparts important 'concepts in action' to the watching child who learns about perseverance, flexibility, error, and the morality of time. Seeing the application of the adult *will (intention, deliberation, perseverance, transformation)*, acts as a model of action for the child's will and the 'happening now' element is a magical tutorial.

Free from the dominance of machines, which are self-sufficient, asocial and set to run at a faster pace than our human one, children are invited but not compelled to join in with the daily activities. They are involved and their contributions are valued. The joy of doing things together, cooking or gardening, for example, awakens the desire to do things for others. The individual *will* easily makes the transition towards becoming a social will.

Slowed-up activities, (such as baking, ironing, washing, cleaning, with their attendant sensory smells, tastes, and textures), form the backdrop to the child's everyday experience. Each one of these processes needs to be slowed up in order to be thorough. Yeast rises in its own time and obeys its own laws. Patience is both a virtue and a necessity where organic processes are concerned. Processes such as these have the effect of rooting children and adults in real time. The patience and delayed gratification involved in bread-making is simply character-building – it absolutely won't be hurried! Celebrating Seasonal Festivals links the child with Natural time and the course of the year. This helps develop healthy respect for the environment, urban and rural, and a feeling for stewardship of the earth.

Natural artefacts: conkers, shells, coloured cloths, pinecones etc., provide wings for the child's *own* imagination to fly-creating an antidote to the borrowed images churned out daily on the box, powerful images which quickly paralyse the individual imagination.

Given time, we know that quite ordinary sensory experiences, even those that are unpleasant, can begin to act as gateways to a rich imaginative life. As a child, R. L. Stevenson was inspired by the contents of his humble breakfast bowl.

When my cousin and I took our porridge of a morning, we had a device to enliven the course of the meal. He ate his with sugar, and explained it to be a country continually buried under snow. I took mine with milk and explained it to be a country suffering gradual inundation. You can imagine us exchanging bulletins; how here there was an island still unsubmerged, here a valley not yet covered with snow; what inventions were made; how his populations lived in cabins on perches and travelled on stilts, and how mine was always in boats; how the interest grew furious, as the last corner of safe ground was cut off on all sides and grew smaller every moment; and how, …the food was of altogether secondary importance, and might have been nauseous, so long as we seasoned it with these dreams.

(Robert Louis Stevenson, quoted in Rosen 1994, p.97)

Fortunately for us, this little boy was not made to 'hurry up.' Though somewhat cavalier about his food, he was given time to live into his present, and here is the mystery again: fully attending the present also serves the future. The first stirrings of the poet and author of the future were present in the wonderful mix of milk, oats, and imagination at his morning breakfast table.

For today's youngsters, the lack of natural rhythm, the presence of so much high-speed activity in computer games, television, videos, etc., leads to over stimulation, dissatisfaction with the present and a disjunction with real time. Medication and certain foods also disturb the child's relationship to time and to the speed at which life is experienced. Children everywhere across the whole social spectrum lack the stabilising influence of healthy habits and daily rhythms. They lack the security that comes from repetition and sameness, the opportunity to experience joy in simple shared tasks and the freedom from the compulsion to perform/conform.

Our children are the future. They need time to create their own visions, to dream their own dreams, and in the fullness of time to act upon them. The least – perhaps the best – we can give them is the gift of the present.

Paper first presented at Parent Child 2000 Conference 12/04/2000, Business Design Centre London

Sally Jenkinson works with the Alliance for Childhood, and is an Early Years Consultant with the UK Steiner Waldorf Schools Fellowship. She was a Kindergarten teacher for many years.

Contact:

Steiner Waldorf Schools Fellowship,
Kidbrooke Park,
Forest Row, East Sussex,
RH18 5JA

E-mail: sallyjenkinson@lineone.net

References

Donaldson, M. *Children's Minds* 1987 Ed. Fontana

Elkind, D. *Miseducation: Pre-schoolers at Risk* 1997 Knopf (orig. 1987)

Eliot, G. *The Mill on the Floss* 1985 Penguin Classics (orig. 1880)

Fromm, E. *To Have or to Be* 1997 Abacus (orig. 1976)

Glöckler, M. (notes from international Conference 'The Young Child', Dornach 1999)

Griffiths, J. *The Morality of Time,* Dartington Easter Conference Paper 1999

Humphries, S., Mack, J., Perks, R. *A Century of Childhood* 1988 Sidgwick&Jackson, London

Large, M. *Out of the Box* 2000 Steiner Education Vol 34 no. 2

Oppenheimer, T. *Schooling the Imagination* 1999 Atlantic Monthly, September issue, 1999

Rosen, M. *The Penguin Book of Childhood* 1994 Viking

Paley, V. G. *The Kindness of Children* 1999 Harvard

The Big Picture, *Bright Futures* Published by the Mental Health Foundation UK, 1999

Struck, Dr. Peter *Movement and Sensory Disorders in Today's Children* published in the Waldorf Education Research Bulletin Vol. IV 1999 (orig.1997)

Vogt, F. *Drugs and Addiction* 2000 Prevention through Education Brochure, International Association of Waldorf Kindergartens Inc., Stuttgart

Winn, M. *The Plug-In Drug* 1985 Penguin Books

Television Statistics

According to the A. C. Nielson Co. (1998), the average American watches 3 hours and 46 minutes of TV each day (more than 52 days of nonstop TV-watching per year). *By the age of 65 the average American will have spent nearly 9 years glued to the tube.*

I. Family Life

1 Percentage of US households with at least one television: 98
2 Percentage of US households with at least one VCR: 84
3 Percentage of US households with two TV sets: 34; three or more TV sets: 40
4 Hours per day that TV is on in an average US home: 7 hours, 12 minutes
5 Percentage of Americans that regularly watch television while eating dinner: 66
6 Number of videos rented daily in the US: 6 million
7 Number of public library items checked out daily: 3 million
8 Chance that an American falls asleep with the TV on at least three nights a week: 1 in 4
9 Percentage of Americans who say they watch too much TV: 49

II. Children and Education

1   Number of minutes per week that the average American child ages 2-11 watches television: 1,197

2   Number of minutes per week that parents spend in meaningful conversation with their children: 38.5

3   Percentage of children ages 5-17 who have a TV in their bedroom: 52

4   Percentage of children ages 2-5 who have a TV in their bedroom: 25

5   Percentage of day care centers that use TV during a typical day: 70

6   Percentage of parents who would like to limit their children's TV watching: 73

7   Percentage of 4-6 year-olds who, when asked to choose between watching TV and spending time with their fathers, preferred television: 54

8   Hours per week of TV watching shown to negatively affect academic achievement: 10 or more

9   Percentage of 4th graders that watch more than 14 hours of television per week: 81

10 Hours per year the average American youth watches television: 1,500

11 Hours per year the average American youth spends in school: 900

12 Chance that an American parent requires that children do their homework before watching TV: 1 in 12

13 Percentage of teenagers 13-17 who can name the city where the US Constitution was written (Philadelphia): 25

14 Percentage of teenagers 13-17 who know where you find the zip code 90210 (Beverly Hills): 75

III. Violence and Health

1 Number of violent acts that the average American child sees on TV by the age 18: 200,000

2 Number of murders witnessed by children on television by the age 18: 16,000

3 Percentage of Hollywood executives who believe there is a link between TV violence and real-life violence: 80

4 Percentage of children polled who said they feel 'upset' or scared by violence on television: 91

5 Percent increase in network news coverage of homicide between 1990 and 1995: 336

6 Percent reduction in the American homicide rate between 1990 and 1995: 13

7 Number of medical studies since 1985 linking excessive television watching to increasing rates of obesity: 12

8 Percentage of American children ages 6 to 11 who were seriously overweight in 1963: 4.5; In 1993: 14

9 Number of ads aired for 'junk-food' during four hours of Saturday morning cartoons: 202

IV. Commercialism

1 Number of TV commercials seen in a year by an average child: 30,000

2 Number of TV commercials seen by the average American by age 65: 2 million

3 Percentage of toy advertising dollars spent on television commercials in 1997: 92

4 Percentage of Americans who believe that 'most of us buy and consume far more than we need': 82

V. General

1 Percentage of local TV news broadcast time devoted to advertising: 30

2 Percentage devoted to stories about crime, disaster and war: 53.8

3 Percentage devoted to public service announcements: 0.7

4 Total amount candidates spent on television ads during the 1996 political campaigns: $2.5 billion

5 Percentage of Americans who can name The Three Stooges: 59

6 Percentage of Americans who can name three Supreme Court Justices: 17

Compiled by TV-Free America, 1611 Connecticut Avenue, NW Suite 3A, Washington, DC 20009 (202) 887-0436

5. The Dot.Com Kids and the Demise of Frustration Tolerance

Marilyn B. Benoit, M.D.

As a practising child and adolescent psychiatrist for the past 25 years, I am observing a disturbing trend in children. I got the idea for the title of this paper from my two and a half year old grand niece, who was very upset when a store clerk prevented her from playing with a display computer. In her anger she complained to her mother, 'He won't let me do www.com!' Recently, when I intervened to stop some unwanted behavior, she dissolved into a crying rage. A delightful, highly verbal child, who is technology savvy for her age, she is not recovering well when she is not immediately gratified. The problem I see emerging in children is one of decreasing frustration tolerance. In lay language, this translates into a lack of patience, that old-fashioned virtue that people of my generation had preached to us repeatedly, 'Patience is a virtue.' I have spent some time pondering this matter, and I have some thoughts I would like to share, hoping to stimulate some serious thinking about this issue.

Psychiatrists are taught that frustration tolerance is an ego strength that human beings need in order to make a successful adaptation to life. While the newborn is entitled to have all its needs met promptly and unconditionally, the developing child is expected to gradually learn to delay gratification as s/he must wait for the parent to produce food, remove a wet diaper, soothe aching gums, play a game, etc. The exponential technological advancements of recent years have afforded the possibility for young children to achieve instant gratification at the touch of a button. An 18 month old can turn on the TV and instantly be entertained by music, dance, interesting shapes and colors, adults, cartoon characters etc. What power for a child who is already in the throes of egocentrism and omnipotence! Technology meets magical thinking and enhances it by making it real. This type of experience is further facilitated by doting parents, who are awed by what their children hear and repeat to them. Every child seems to be a budding genius! No self respecting parent wants his/her child to be left behind, so the child gets the computer toys and a personal computer with all the 'intelligence enhancing' software that is peddled to parents nowadays. Parents provide increasingly more elaborate video games, TV's and entertainment centers in their children's rooms, where the kids can cocoon themselves in their multimedia environment. Those same kids go to the ATM with the parent and see real money emerge from a machine with the use of a plastic card and the touch of some buttons. While most children cannot appreciate the fact that many work hours are needed to provide the money so easily retrieved from the ATM, the easy availability and accessibility of cash distance them even further from that concept.

Many children are now on the Internet receiving almost instant responses to queries. Groups can form instant 'chat rooms,' creating rapid virtual social gatherings. A recent cartoon by Mike Twohy in the Washington Post (1/11/00) depicted a young boy leaving the family dinner table in anger while shouting 'Fine – I'll go talk to my chat room family!' This indeed captures the sense that he no longer has to tolerate whatever discomfort and frustration he experienced with his family. The instant solution is available through the capability of technology to readily substitute a new social entity and gratify his perceived needs. The emerging mantra of this technological era is 'wait no more!' The ubiquitous cell phone can provide instant communication with each other. I recall that as a child, I would wait about one month with heightened anticipation to receive a reply from my pen pal in England. Now e-mail and instant messaging have created an expectation of rapid communication. What has ensued is the experience of *impatience* (poor frustration tolerance) when the response does not come in the anticipated brief turnaround time. We must concede that the rapidity of these technological changes, and their impact on our youngsters must have significant influence upon the ways kids perceive, experience and adapt to their world. Of course, most of the effect of modern day technology is beneficial, but we must give pause to at least be mindful of potential long term negative impacts upon the psychological and social development of our children.

It is only 50 years since Erik Erickson wrote *Childhood and Society*, in which he discussed the stages of child development. The family played a major role in filtering and modulating the interplay between the developing child and society's influences. With technology, that role has not only changed, but it has definitely diminished. The protected 'autosphere' of the child's early world in the home nursery has now been invaded and bombarded by TV images and computer software. Children now live in an ecology of technology. The gradual transition described by Erickson from the child's autosphere to the social macrosphere no longer exists. The brain of the young child is overstimulated by the new multimedia environment with its sound effects, and rapidly changing, attention-grabbing images. I do wonder about the effect on the attention span of the developing brain. Could the rise in case finding of Attention Deficit Hyperactivity

Disorder be related to children's constant exposure to rapid-fire stimuli on their brains? *(As I write, I am impressed by my use of war-related terminology: invaded, bombarded, rapid-fire. Has war been declared on the brain? And have parents, as protectors, abdicated?)* Is it possible that, (given our new insights into brain development and brain and behavior), different neural pathways and changing neurotransmitter levels and combinations are developing?

It is intriguing that the very parents who expose their children to the new technologies, in an effort to provide the best for them, seem oblivious to the possible impact on the developing child's mind and his/her social behavior. If one has been raised to have instant gratification, is it then surprising that at those times when one has to wait one's turn, be left out, or not get a desired object, explosive rage is the result? Frustration is a feeling state that emanates from our innate aggression. If it cannot be tolerated, aggression in words or in deeds is the result. In the developing child, frustration tolerance increases as the parents withhold instant gratification in 'doses' that are manageable for the child's level of development. This allows the child the opportunity to learn to manage his/her feelings of frustration, and develop coping skills to manage them. The child learns to do without some things, and to be patient and wait for others. S/he also learns to give up his/her egocentrism and magical thinking during the process. Primary narcissism is tamed. S/he has to then take in the bigger world around him/her and develop tolerance of people and of situations. Tolerance requires the development of empathy. And empathy requires time to think about another person while putting aside one's own needs or wishes. Children's early use of the new technologies is causing a profound change in how they experience the passage of time, and they are less willing to wait for what they perceive as long periods of time.

I am impressed by the apparent link between technology, instant gratification, poor frustration tolerance, lack of empathy and aggression. While I do not propose that technology is the 'cause' of the episodes of horrific violence we have seen in young people in recent years, I do think that we should be mindful of some of the negative impacts of our new technologies. As with all technological advances, these are unintended consequences which should raise some concern, especially at a time in our history when parents are spending less time with their children, and do not serve as much of a protective function as they once did. Psychiatry teaches that it is both nurturing and limit setting from parents that neutralize aggression in the young child. I contend that the combination of decreased parental protection and increased instant gratification changes the psychology and undermines the socialization of the developing child. When frustration tolerance is not acquired, modulation and management of aggression is compromised, and we see children like those who are now labeled 'explosive' children. Excluding those children with neurobiological deficits, psychiatry describes such children as 'narcissistic' and their explosiveness as 'narcissistic rage.' They are children who are unable to cope with the slightest of frustrations, and lash out aggressively. They are entitled, demanding, impatient, disrespectful of authority, often contemptuous of their peers, unempathic and easily 'wounded.' Their numbers are increasing. We must take note of this disturbing trend and intervene with some urgency if we are to raise children who will care about others in society.

I have been fascinated by the role nature can play in developing frustration tolerance. Perhaps we can temper the negative technological impacts by taking children on excursions into nature where they can spend time observing the plants and animals, pondering the rivers and lakes, and marveling at the ocean. What frustration tolerance it takes to go fishing or to do birdwatching! With all our technological advancements, the sun still rises and sets in a twenty-four hour cycle, we must wait out the drought or the hurricane, contend with snow storms shutting down airports and the nation's capital, wait for crops to grow, for flowers to bloom, for seasons to change. For all of those, indeed 'Patience is a virtue!'

6. Brain Development and Montessori Theory – The Links

Helen Prochazka, PhD

Introduction

This is the decade of the brain, and recent technological advances, particularly computer-based brain imaging techniques, have been pushing back the frontiers of knowledge about the structure, development and workings of the human brain. These discoveries have had a high media profile, and the starting point for this article was a growing awareness that much of what was being reported seemed to come as no surprise to Montessori practitioners.

To investigate why this should be so I revisited Montessori's thinking on the brain in the light of current research. The models described below, I venture to suggest, have implications for our work with children in the early years.

I would like to make clear that the brain is not my field of expertise, and I am not in a position to evaluate the research in question. All I have attempted to do in this article is to indicate how some recent discoveries seem to link with the Montessori understanding of the processes of mental development, and at this point I should like briefly to set out a historical context for the remarks which follow.

Maria Montessori lived from 1870 to 1952, and was an educationist, rather than a psychologist. She approached her work from a strong scientific background of clinical observation gained from her medical studies and subsequent academic career in mental health. She applied her observational skills to the children she was working with, and from what she observed she gradually elaborated her theories of child development and education which she supported with reference to the research of the day. Montessori was first and foremost a practitioner, engaged in what today we would call 'active research'. Her theories followed on from her observations.

Montessori's structural model

The structural model of brain development elaborated by Maria Montessori was based on a rooted conviction that, starting from the moment of birth, the infant is hard at work, actively constructing the very substance of his psyche. By 'psyche' she meant everything pertaining to the child that was non-physical: cognitive abilities, personality, character, emotions, spirituality and social tendencies.

She considered that the child was possessed of 'a true constructive energy, a dynamic power' and speaks of the child undertaking 'an impressive work of inner formation' (1988). Her whole approach to her work was underpinned by the belief that the most important period of life is not the age of university studies, but '...the period from birth to the age of six. For that is the time when man's intelligence itself, his greatest implement, is being formed. But not only his intelligence, the full totality of his psychic powers.' (1988:21)

Her observations convinced her that the child started from nothing and created: 'We are not dealing with something that develops, but with a fact of formation, something non-existent that has to be produced, starting from nothing…' (1988:21) but she also emphasised that this process of construction for the first three years of life was essentially a hidden one, continuing predominantly unobserved and unobservable by adults. She saw this, coupled with the understanding that the child's psyche is completely unlike that of the adult, as the key to what she termed 'the secret of childhood.'

The analogy she devised to explain her conception of how the child's psyche develops was the 'spiritual embryo', a vivid image which encompasses the idea of inexorability, miraculous growth and sudden emergence, as if newly born, into a form comprehensible to adults. Just as the physical embryo develops unseen in the womb, to appear fully formed at birth, Maria Montessori saw the emerging psychological traits of the child as the embryonic form of the spirit, born ready for future development in an adult-orientated and adult-directed world at around three. She felt that the period before the age of three was inaccessible to adults to safeguard the integrity of the structural process: 'He has the chance to build up a complete psychic structure before the intelligence of grownups can reach his spirit and produce changes in it.' (1988:6)

The emphasis placed by Montessori on construction is borne out by recent discoveries about the workings of the brain. We now know that the many millions of neurons, or nerve cells in the brain, possibly as many as ten billion, function together, to transmit, or inhibit nerve impulses. The main channels for the firing of the impulses are the axons, sheathed in myelin, like long, insulation-covered wires. Also extending from each cell are varying numbers of dendrites, branched like trees, in arrangements that may be fairly simple, or in great profusion. Through its dendrites the neuron receives messages from sense organs, or from other neurons, combines and processes the information, and responds by either increasing or decreasing the pulses of electricity it passes down the axon.

The electrical impulses cause a flow of chemicals to cross the gap at the end of the axon to the next neuron, so passing a message on. The gaps between the axons and dendrites of different neurons, the synapses, appear to function like valves controlling the message flow, sifting, sorting and combining as part of the tissue of communication pathways. The numbers are mind-boggling – some neurons may have as many as 20,000 synapses on their dendrites. A small one might only have 2,000.

The neurons do not act individually, but in concert with thousands, if not hundreds of thousands of others, together either activating, or inhibiting the transmission of the electrical and chemical impulses. The process of transmitting impulses has been likened to the action of waves, a simile which allows the description of impulses that flow off at a tangent, waves that divide, fleetingly joining other waves to create incredibly complex, possibly abortive, patterns before subsiding. Not surprisingly, fifty years ago the nearest Montessori came to describing this amazingly complex process was to say 'a kind of mental chemistry goes on within him.' (1988:24)

What is particularly interesting, however, for the present discussion, is to consider the processes by which the connections between the cells, through the synapses, are formed. It is now known that these pathways are established in response to stimuli, and strengthened through repetition.

Studies of brain growth reveal spurts of growth at different stages of development. The first short spurt of very rapid growth is in the womb, between 12 and 18 weeks. This is when the neurons multiply to their adult number when the baby is probably least influenced by external factors. The responses of the foetal brain to changes in sound, light and touch were uncharted in Montessori's day, but today we know that the brain is active before birth.

At birth the brain comprises about 14 percent of the baby's total body weight, compared with 2 percent in the adult, but this equates to twenty five percent of its adult weight. The major growth spurt occurs between the 6th month of pregnancy and the age of 2, evidenced by the fact that at 6 months the brain is about fifty percent of its adult weight, and by two and a half, seventy five percent. Growth is still very swift until around five years when it has reached about 90 percent of its adult weight in comparison with a body weight of about half its adult value. Brain growth continues steadily, if less fast, until the age of about 10, when it is about ninety five percent of its final adult weight.

During the major growth spurt in the first two years the neurons are developing their dendrites, their synaptic connections, and the myelin sheaths of the nerve fibres, the axons, without which impulses cannot be conducted.

The myelinisation process of the part of the brain controlling physical movement, the motor cortex, is something which begins to happen a few months after birth. The motor nerve fibres are not able to conduct impulses until their myelin sheaths are in place, and so a full range of movement is not possible. This delay is seen as essential for survival, to enable the infant to acquire a working perception of his world before he begins to be mobile in it. Aware of this physiological process Montessori asserted: '...there are psychic patterns of behaviour which have to be laid down before he begins to move. Thus the starting point of infant mobility is not motor, but mental.' (1988:66)

Montessori's process model

Montessori's process model is based on the idea that a child between the ages of birth and six has what she termed an 'absorbent mind'. To explain this she used the analogy of a sponge, and proposed a model of learning whereby the child absorbed impressions from the environment surrounding him. This was by no means passive absorption, however. Her model is predicated on a complex interrelationship between the child's emergent psyche, the spur to learning presented by stimuli from the environment, and the challenge the child instinctively sets himself in order to acquire the learning. This is what we might term, on a conscious level, 'finding the problem'. It is precisely this idea of finding the problem that has been instrumental over the last 25 years in extending definitions of intelligence. (Hatch and Gardener, 1996:90).

In this process of absorbing impressions the *elan vital*, the vital urge or life force, plays a key role. This is an overpowering force which drives the human being from the moment of conception to develop and grow, ensuring he or she is in learning mode. This is the force which activates the brain's potentialities, termed by Montessori 'nebulae' or clouds, an image she drew from astronomy to convey her conception of as yet formless swirling masses, representing the infinite potential of the forming mind.

Perhaps we can equate her nebulae to the neural architectures that contemporary cognitive neuroscience sees the genes providing for the brain. It is not yet fully understood how the genes affect the definition of the functional areas of the brain, and although these are pre-ordained, the very plastic nature of the brain for the first few years of life means that the functional areas can be reconfigured. The human genome is underspecified in terms of allocating function, but it seems as though different types of neural architectures are suited for different tasks, with propensities to be different specialists.

In the Montessori model, because the child's brain is actively receptive to ever present stimuli from the environment, the clouds of potentialities, the propensities, are switched on to learning mode by the life force. The child is thus impelled to interact with the environment and sets about mastering it and incarnating it. '...the things he sees are not just remembered; they form part of his soul.' (1988:56)

Speaking of the nervous system as the 'liaison' between the inner needs of the body and the external environment, Sillick emphasises that it is '*not* a simple stimulus-response affair. It is a constant two-way communication between the body and the external world, from inner to outer and back to the inner world... The information transaction between the organism and its environment, as it increases quantitatively and qualitatively, results in the capacity for learning.' (1996:84)

But why should the child respond to one particular stimulus rather than another? Here we need to focus on the idea of the individual being predisposed to receive the stimulus and act upon it, being pre-programmed, as if the child's hard disk is already configured to respond to a particular stimulus at a particular time. For example, research has shown that within 30 minutes of birth a baby can distinguish between the phonemes [b] and [p], an ability that lasts until the age of about a year, and plays a key role in language acquisition. It is also the case that if the same stimulus appears at a different time, one that is not optimal for learning, it will not trigger such intensity of response, and then the learning that takes place will be less efficient, less focused, less effective.

We are talking here of the 'critical periods', 'windows of opportunity' for optimal learning that are now identified by cognitive neuroscientists. Ninety years ago Maria Montessori described them as 'sensitive periods' and observed their effects, as the children in her care, predisposed to learn, armed with nebulous potentialities, and highly sensitive to stimuli in the environment displayed fixed determination to engage in an activity, or pursue an interest to the point of adult exasperation and lack of patience.

For Montessori these sensitivities were the key to understanding how the child's mind is formed. She was quite clear that 'it is not the mind itself that these sensitivities create, but its *organs*'

(1988:47) and that this form of sensitivity was so intense as to lead the child to perform a specific series of actions over and over again in concerted focus.

This phenomenon can be explained now that the function of repetition in brain development is acknowledged as the means whereby connections established and used become significantly strengthened. If they are not, they are lost. The sensitive periods of the Montessori model are passed through in order. Each sensitivity is specifically focused and disappears once the relevant mental development has occurred. Sometimes they overlap, and they vary in length according to the individual child. They are universal. They occur in all children, and the external manifestations are indicative of the great internal development taking place unseen. 'It is these 'inner sensitivities', the sensitive periods, which enable the absorbent mind to construct itself.' (Montessori, 1989:61)

That the construction of the mind is an unconscious process is obvious when we contrast the outward indications of the workings of the child's mind with those of the adult's. Adults bring to bear attention, will power and intelligence to their activities. The infant has not yet developed his intelligence, has a very limited attention span compared with a grown-up, and has no will-power as yet. The inescapable conclusion is that the mind of a child under three is completely different from that of an adult. This led Maria Montessori to conclude that: 'a psychic functioning different from that of the conscious mind can exist in the unconscious.' (1989:61)

At what point does the unconscious mind become conscious? According to Susan Greenfield 'the more complex the brain, the greater the consciousness'. The three properties inherent in Greenfield's definition of consciousness help us to explain the change. If consciousness does indeed result from concerted activity by neurons located in different areas of the brain in response to some stimulus, and if it is the sum of the unspecialised neurons working together, the degree of consciousness will depend on how many neurons are entrained around some kind of epicentre (1998:214). Her stone in the puddle image helps us to visualise the ripples of neurons extending outwards from the epicentre it represents.

But what does she mean by 'epicentre'? Again we come back to neuronal connections in the brain, because Greenfield sees the epicentres as 'circuits of neurons' that refer to the outside world, neurons where connections have already been established that give great flexibility and versatility to moments of consciousness. Giving childhood as an example of small neuronal assemblies because of limited connections leads her to suggest that 'less mature brains are much more dominated by whatever epicentre is triggered from the outside', and leads her to conclude, mirroring Montessori, 'the immature brain in the first year of life, and to a certain extent in the further 9 years, is very different from our adult waking brains.' (1998:222).

Profiling the type of consciousness that would be characteristic of a small child Greenfield speaks of 'raw phenomenal consciousness …an absorbing awareness of the outside world… One would not have a lot of 'internal resources' of reflection and memories and thoughts.' (1998:225)

The change from 'unconscious' to 'conscious' is a gradual process happening as the child grows and brain connections are made, but accumulated observation by Montessorians over many years, and in all parts of the world, identifies a marked, often very sudden transition from one phase of mental development and thinking process to another at around the age of three years. It is as if all the parts of a symphony practised separately until now suddenly come together, and a thinking person emerges.

It seems to us that the key to this change is to do with the development of a reliable memory. Most adults have very few recollections pre-dating their third birthday, but can remember clearly incidents in their lives from 3 onwards, another sign that there has been a change in the psychological processes around this time. With a more effective memory it becomes possible to sort and categorise information. It seems that this is the focus that the thinking of three year olds takes, as they set about eliciting huge quantities of information and language from adults in response to their endless 'Why?' questions.

Even though the thinking processes are becoming conscious the critical, or sensitive periods still continue, and the stimuli from the environment are still the trigger. What kind of stimuli are we talking about? They seem to be multi-sensory, and probably strike the child in the same way as, for example, if you begin to think of buying a particular model of new car, you suddenly see them everywhere, or if you become interested in Thai cuisine, in the supermarket you are drawn to shelves of ingredients that you never even noticed previously.

For the last several years Montessori educators have been examining their approach in the light of Howard Gardener's theory of multiple intelligences. He defines intelligence as 'uncommitted neurobiological *potentials* for processing particular kinds of information' (in Wharburton, 1999:220). Many of his findings resonate with what Montessorians know from observation, although an obstacle to complete congruence of ideas lies in the Montessori conviction that the unity of the personality is paramount, that all aspects of the child's psyche combine to form a whole self, a soul, that is balanced and harmonious, at one with all aspects of the environment surrounding it, and developing and growing to realise its full potential in all areas.

It is important, therefore, that we extend Montessori understanding of how children's minds work by superimposing Gardener's ideas on our own, to create a working overlay for closer examination of key aspects of children's intelligence focused on by Maria Montessori. I propose to touch briefly on three of these, namely the mathematical mind, the hand as the instrument of the mind, and the social embryo.

Montessori's observations led her to put forward the view that small children have 'a mathematical mind', a term she adopted from the French philosopher Pascal (1988:169). She recorded the reactions of a 4 week old baby seeing his father and his uncle together for the first time. He had seen them both separately on previous occasions, but was startled and unsettled by seeing them together for the first time. They reassured him by separating, and standing apart from each other. The baby kept looking from one to the other seemingly until he was secure in his understanding of the fact that there were two men, and not just the one he had previously encountered (1966:61-62). Montessori cited this as an example of the beginnings of reasoning, but in the light of recent research into infant numerosity it can equally well be attributed to 'dishabituation', or stirring of interest by novelty. (Butterworth 1999:112-116).

Butterworth and his colleagues have demonstrated the existence of the mathematical brain, and so, armed with this definitive understanding, as educators we can now be more confident in interpreting our observations of children. But to look only for very early awareness of number is, I think, too limiting. And this is where Gardener's definition of logical / mathematical intelligence is one to consider closely (Hatch and Gardener, 1996), allied as it is to Montessori's comment that precision itself seemed to hold the children's interest, and that order and precision were the keys to spontaneous work (1988:169).

Let's consider next Montessori's adage 'the hands are the instruments of man's intelligence'. Traditionally this has been taken to mean that through the progressive refinement of the movements of the hand learning took place. In the light of what we now know about how the brain is formed this becomes infinitely more significant, because of the brain being actually constructed through movement. The great importance that the hand plays in mental development and learning is borne out by the much larger areas of the motor cortex concerned with manual dexterity that can now be shown by brain imaging techniques. Montessori insisted on the need to educate the functioning of the hand, to develop its movement, and on a larger scale to guard against separating body from mind in the curriculum for fear of breaking 'the continuity that should reign between them' (1988:130). She identified a sensitive period for movement lasting from birth to 6, critical for the development of the mind, because, to quote Sillick, 'the child's movement of his or her whole body prepares the neural pathways for cognitive development, language acquisition and creative expression...' (1996:85). Again this resonates with Gardener's visual/spatial awareness, and bodily kinesthetic intelligences. (Hatch and Gardener, 1996)

The notion of the 'social embryo', an analogy similar to the spiritual embryo already described, summarises the Montessori view of the child's social development and his growing awareness of self. Again we are dealing with an individual in the process of growing and maturing towards adult norms of behaviour. Again development is directly bound to processes of construction in the mind.

In his reflections on the development of consciousness, and the neurobiological processes involved, Singer concludes that one's awareness of self arises only through the interaction of one's own brain with the brains of others. He says, 'the experience of one's own individuality, the ability to experience oneself as an autonomous individual with subjective feelings – is to be seen as the result of social interactions, and hence of cultural evolution' (1998:242).

Human interaction with the baby starts from birth, and the neural mechanisms for self-awareness are likely to be developed before the brain is mature enough to remember and recall anything of this process. Furthermore, the process is unrepeatable because as it happens it directly influences the way the processing structures of the brain develop. Singer concludes that 'the specific human connotations of consciousness are likely to be the product of cultural evolution', and suggests that the subjective mental aspects of consciousness are the result of a social learning process (1998:242). This thinking echoes Montessori's conviction that '...there exists in this inert being a global power, a 'human creative essence' which drives him to form a man of his time, a man of his civilisation'. She signposted the way for Singer and others when she asserted that this was a 'progress unaided by any hereditary transmission of acquired characteristics.' (1988:53)

At birth the infant is totally dependent on his parents to meet all his needs, whereas by six he has attained a degree of functional independence and is increasingly aware of himself as a social individual. We need to remember that the degree of social autonomy children can aspire to is culturally conditioned. It depends where and when they are born as to where and when, and the degree to which they become able to reconcile their needs as individuals with their responsibilities as members of society. The first years of life are the formative ones in this regard, when the child soaks up information about the culture and social norms prevalent in the society in which he lives. He is very much of his place and time, as Montessori emphasised.

The implications for education

Given that Montessori's observations, and the models developed from them can now be substantiated in this way, it seems there is merit in reevaluating the educational approach that she developed in response to what she observed, and in particular its theoretical underpinnings.

The concept of the prepared environment is fundamental. Early years educators all recognise the significance of quality settings for effective early learning. Montessori practitioners take this further. They aim to perfect a learning environment that will meet the needs of all children, as individuals, regardless of the stage of learning they are at. The environment must 'call' to the children, it must actively engage their interest, it must be accessible to them, fresh, stimulating, clearly seen, uncluttered and, above all beautiful, for it appeals to the innermost depths of the developing soul. The environment provides the stimulus that is seized on by those nebulous potentialities for learning.

Crucially the child has to be free within the environment, free from time constraints, free from pressure to learn, free from competition. Each individual must be free to choose whatever interests him, to do with it as his inspiration directs, and for as long or as short a time as he instinctively feels is necessary.

The life of the small child, particularly his intellectual life, has an ebbing and flowing pace that does not harmonise well with the hectic lives of today's parents. Unconsciously driven by his learning urge the child has no concept of appropriate time and place. He is impelled to reach out and explore all the manifestly exciting and fascinating aspects of his environment without conscious thought. His whims are not rational, in an adult understanding of the term. They are clues to the current sensitive period and need to be understood and examined as such. And it is important to understand that he is soaking up all aspects of his environment, not just the positive learning experiences carefully arranged for him, but everything around him: language, behaviour, attitudes, prejudices. He is enthused, enamoured of, addicted to his environment. He loves what he finds there, and however humble and seemingly insignificant his interests and preoccupations, they are the very matter of his mind – through his activity in the environment he is building his intellect, his emotions, his personality. Montessori summarised the process: 'The immense influence that education can exert through children has the environment for its instrument, for the child absorbs his environment, takes everything from it, and incarnates it in himself.' (1988:61)

People are a key part of this environment, and for the social embryo to develop fully the infant needs to be a valued part of the social scene. Research shows how her language develops best when she is surrounded by adults communicating with each other, and with her, from the earliest days of life. As an active observer privy to the everyday rituals of living she soaks up the culture of the time and place that is her own, and the adults in the environment can enrich her experiences by being with her. There is no need to do way out and costly things, nor overly 'educational' or 'fun' things. As adults we need 'to be there for her', or more accurately, 'with her', sharing her small experiences rather than trying to inflict our own on her. In the same way that going for a walk with a child should not mean dragging her along at the brisk pace of our adult legs to get to a certain place by a certain time, but rather covering a unspecified distance in an unspecified length of time at the child's pace and in response to her interests, on the social front the same is true. Because socially she is in embryonic form until she is about 6 and because her emergent skills and abilities here are still far from those expected by the adult, more than anything she needs to proceed at her own pace. And more than anything, as adults, we need to be sure that we are not putting obstacles in her way.

The first six years of life are often an obstacle course with major hurdles placed in the way by well-intentioned adults. Among these we can list pressure to achieve ('He knows his alphabet and can count'), pressure to act in a socially acceptable way ('Share your toys!'), to be quick ('Come on, hurry up!'), to be dragged away from what actively interests him... to have things done for him that he is well able to do for himself... It is likely that such pressures create stress in the small child. The stress hormone cortisol kills brain cells. The adults in the environment need to observe the child, so as to be able to meet his needs, to give support where necessary, but mostly to stand back to let him get to grips with his environment by himself, on his own terms, in safety and security.

Montessori practice values very highly the skill of 'active observation, the ability to be there, involved with the children as a sympathetic facilitator, as part of the environment, but not interrupting or diverting the flow of activity. Flow, a psychological state identified by Csikszentmihalyi, is characterised by Goleman as representing 'perhaps the ultimate in harnessing the emotions in the service of performance and learning... it is intrinsically rewarding... a state in which people become utterly absorbed in what they are doing... their awareness merged with their actions' (1996:90-91).

This concept is specially familiar to Montessorians who are continually on the look-out for this phenomenon, because it is a sign that all the aspects of the child's personality and psyche are fusing, that he has discovered the capacity for concentration on purposive and intentioned activity, and we can see when this happens that it refreshes his soul.

Montessori repeatedly spoke of the education of movement, and the connection between movement and brain development is now well-established. Everything in the environment should encourage different kinds of independent movement. All the activities to be freely chosen by the children should be selected for the environment because of the motor activity they encourage. And always there should be the opportunity to repeat... as often as the child desires.

And yet, how often do we interrupt a small child, considering his activity inferior in importance to our own? Each time an adult says, 'We can't wait here all day. You'll have to stop now. You can do it another time' the child's brain development is being obstructed, diminished. As educators we should be specially sensitive to this and strive consciously to follow Montessori's example of never interrupting a child who is experiencing 'flow'.

Helen Prochazka was born in Glasgow, Scotland. She has a PhD in Russian, a PGCE in post-compulsory education and training, and both foundation and advanced Montessori Diplomas. She is also an NVQ assessor for Early Years Care and Education awards.

Combining a research background in mediaeval Russian with a variety of teaching experiences in the UK and the Middle East, Helen first became involved in the early years when teaching in the English-medium kindergarten of an Arabic school. Introduced by a colleague to the educational ideas of Montessori she embarked on training, and was eventually appointed Director of Studies for the St Nicholas Montessori Training Centre. Now, as a partner of the Montessori Partnership she is involved setting up and quality-assuring Montessori teacher training programmes, she co-owns two Montessori nurseries, one of which she manages directly, and she is currently the Chairman of the national umbrella body for Montessori, Montessori Education UK. She writes on Montessori and the early years.

Contact:

1 Brooklyn Close, Otterbourne,
Winchester SO21 2EF
Tel/fax: 01962 715675
E-mail: HYPH@aol.com

References

Butterworth, B. 1999, *The Mathematical Brain,* Macmillan.

Goleman, D. 1996, *Emotional Intelligence: Why It Can Matter More Than IQ,* Bloomsbury.

Greenfield, S. 1998, 'How Might the Brain Generate Consciousness?' in Rose, S. (ed), *From Brains to Consciousness? Essays on the New Science of the Mind,* Allen Lane Penguin pp. 210-227.

Hatch, T. & Gardener, H. 1996, 'If Binet Had Looked beyond the Classroom', *The NAMTA Journal,* Vol. 21, No 2, pp. 5-28.

Montessori, M. 1988, *The Absorbent Mind,* Clio Press, Oxford.

Montessori, M. 1989, *The Formation of Man,* Clio Press, Oxford.

Montessori, M. 1972, *The Secret of Childhood,* Ballantine, New York.

Sillick, A. 1996, 'Movement, Music and Learning: the Musical and Bodily/Kinesthetic Intelligences', *The NAMTA Journal,* Vol. 21, No 2, pp. 81-96.

Singer, W. 1998, 'Consciousness from a Neurobiological Perspective', in Rose, S. (ed), *From Brains to Consciousness? Essays on the New Science of the Mind,* Allen Lane Penguin pp. 228-245

Wharburton, E. 1999, 'Multiple Intelligences: Past, Present, Future', *The NAMTA Journal,* Vol. 24, No. 1, pp. 209-223.

7. The Children of the 21st Century

Joan Almon

We stand at the edge of a new century and new millennium. For today's children and youth it will be 'home'. They will feel themselves more a part of the 21st century than the 20th, and their gifts for this life will be put to use in the next century rather than the past one. Who are these young people of the 21st century? How can we understand their gifts and their struggles?

Today's children and youth are full of contrasting – and sometimes puzzling – qualities. Writers in the United States call them Generation X, the 'x' standing for mysterious and unknown. Now they are being recognized as an amazing generation, and the press says the 'x' stands for extraordinary and exceptional! They are known to be unusually caring and compassionate about the earth and about human beings. Even at young ages, today's children want to devote themselves to helping others.

There are remarkable stories of children creating large international organizations to be of service to others. One such young person is Craig Kielburger of Toronto. At age 12 he was so moved by the story of a Pakistani child chained to a rug loom all day, that he traveled with a mentor through India and Pakistan meeting child laborers. He then created an international organization for helping such children called Free the Children. Today Craig is 17 years old. Last year we invited Craig to address Waldorf teachers in North America and asked him to speak about youth today. His words live strongly in me. He said, if you do not help today's children serve others by the time they are 10 or 11, you will lose them to the shopping malls. By this he meant that materialism will grab hold of the children unless we find ways to help them serve others, which is their greatest wish.

This is the wonderful, even awe-inspiring side of today's youth. But there is another side to their lives, as well. Within the economically developed countries, and increasingly around the globe, this generation has been heavily influenced by a growing commercialism that shows little concern for human life or the well-being of the earth. As a result, large numbers of children suffer from illnesses which are relatively new to childhood and which are growing rapidly like an epidemic around the world. What are these conditions that so influence childhood today?

In the United States we saw the first signs of danger in the 1970s when it became evident that children were becoming very nervous and stressed. One U.S. psychologist, David Elkind, described in his book, *The Hurried Child*, that he was seeing far more children under stress in his clinical practice than he had seen before. In general, they came from hurried homes with a hurried lifestyle where children were expected to function as if they were much older than they were. For a long time it seemed this was an American problem, but in recent years the same conditions have spread to Europe and elsewhere, and one sees more and more children under stress. European press articles, for example, speak of growing mental illness in children, growing language problems and a rapid increase in obesity, among other problems. The latter is generally related to a sedentary lifestyle – too many hours spent in front of television, video and computer screens.

and this is the school. Here, too, one sees growing problems for children. At a Waldorf conference recently, a school doctor from Holland spoke of schools being sanctuaries for children, safe places where they can grow and develop. Unfortunately, too often schools have become places of stress for children rather than sanctuaries.

To some extent this has always been so, but today, as pressure grows for children to learn more at an earlier age, the stress has increased greatly. In the United States, for example, kindergartens today are radically different from those of 30 years ago. Then children could play and do artistic work and perhaps receive a mild introduction to the alphabet and numbers. Today the state requires that children master the beginnings of reading *before* they enter first grade, not during first grade as previously. To help them attain this goal, five year olds must stop playing and concentrate on the basics of writing and reading. Yet children's rate of development has not changed significantly. They become ready for reading and other academic studies between ages six and seven. Then and now it has been the same. Demanding that they read at five does not change their pace of development. It only adds stress to their lives.

The assumption, of course, is that this early learning will give children a head start in life that will be beneficial to them and to society. Yet after 30 years of pushing primary school education into the kindergartens and nursery schools, there is no evidence that early academics help children. Indeed, there is evidence that starting children too early with writing, reading and arithmetic may slow them down mentally, as well as emotionally and physically.

In Germany, in the 1970's, there was great enthusiasm about early academics. Play-oriented kindergartens were being rapidly transformed into academic programs. Then a study was done of 50 play-oriented kindergartens and 50 academic kindergartens. The children were followed until fourth grade when it was shown that the children from the play-oriented kindergartens did better than those in the academic kindergartens in every area measured – physical, emotional, social and mental development. The results were so convincing that the German government changed all the kindergartens back into play-oriented kindergartens. Yet in countries like the United States, the trend towards academic work for four and five year olds continues to escalate. The entry of computers into kindergartens only intensifies the emphasis on academic learning more fully. The result is that children spend far less time playing and developing oral language and social skills. There is growing concern about how difficult it is for many children to learn to read. Yet parents, educators and policy makers are unwilling or unable to look at the fundamental problem: that education is no longer based on a sound picture of child development.

Throughout the world there are also positive examples of education well-suited to a child's healthy development. I am most familiar with Waldorf education, for I have worked with Waldorf early childhood education for nearly 30 years. In Waldorf education we seek to understand child development and allow that reality to stand behind all decisions on curriculum and school life. The teachers are greatly helped by the deep insights into child and human development offered by Rudolf Steiner, the founder of Waldorf education.

In addition to providing appropriate education for children, Waldorf schools also stress healthy lifestyles for the home. The fruits of this were revealed recently in a Swedish study comparing several hundred Waldorf students with a comparable number of state school children. All lived in the same town and were of similar social and economic background. Yet the state school children showed far more signs of allergies than did the Waldorf children, and the researchers concluded that a wide array of factors were at work. The Waldorf children tended to be less immunized than the other children, they relied less on antibiotics, their diet was healthier as was their overall lifestyle. The researchers concluded that the more 'Steiner units' in a child's life, the less allergy was present.

The impetus for founding the Alliance for Childhood originally came from Waldorf educators and school doctors. They witnessed the steady decline in children's health and felt they must reach out to parents, educators, health professionals, researchers and child advocates who cared about the well-being of children and were deeply concerned about the current trends. Out of a series of meetings the Alliance for Childhood was born, a partnership of individuals and organizations who work together on a variety of issues. The mission of the Alliance is to focus on the difficulties children face and bring about social change so that all children will have the opportunity for a sound childhood.

For more information about the Alliance work, one can visit a website at: www.allianceforchildhood.net

or write to: Alliance for Childhood, P.O. Box 444, College Park, MD 20741, USA
or in Europe at: 18 Heubergstr., D-70188 Stuttgart, Germany.

Joan Almon is co-chair of the Waldorf Early Childhood Association of North America and a founding partner of the Alliance for Childhood.

Contact:

E-mail: JAlmon@erols.com

8. Out of the Box

Martin Large

Do you suffer from information fatigue syndrome? Consider your daily bombardment by television, e-mail, news, faxes and advertising. On average we are exposed to 2500 advertising messages each day, a deluge of information. At the same time there is the rise of such TV and computer related phenomena as RSI, stress, eye strain, couch potatoes, childhood obesity, attention deficit disorder and other learning disabilities. Even Ted Turner, of CNN said at the launch of his new Customs News service, that the information smog had gone too far, saying, 'It's killing people'.

And there is more to come as technology becomes ever more sophisticated, prices fall and access widens. Over 70% children in Britain have TVs and videos in their bedrooms. Consider the widespread use of hand held video games, CD Roms and internetted computers, the arrival of potentially 200 digital TV channels and hand held mobile telephone/computers!

One conclusion from all this is that the information technologies are no longer part of our environment: they *are* the environment for many people. An event does not really happen unless it is on TV. And there are huge battles going on for commercial dominance of TV and the internet, as companies realise the power of these electronic media 'to deliver people's minds'. The dizzy rise of the share prices of loss-making internet companies shows the stakes are high.

Yet, there is also a gathering backlash against the electronic media and their cultural domination. Whilst useful and enjoyable on occasion, computers and TV can be so boring, 'a medium for muggles' rather than wizards as Harry Potter might say! Children *love* good stories – *Harry Potter* has sold over 27 million! And let's own up, we all love stories, and perhaps this explains some of the mesmeric effect of television. As Thomas Moore writes, 'We are a people in desperate need of stories, so needy that we don't care much about the value of the story, as long as it absorbs our attention and stirs our emotions.'

So, storytelling is making a big comeback all over the Western world, together with puppetry, the visual and the performing arts. One reason for this is that parents and teachers are saying it's not good enough to talk about the impact of the electronic, commercial media on our children, to sit around TV bashing! So, for example, some Pine Hill Waldorf School parents have created an annual Fathers Day festival on the third Sunday in June for families, called the Joseph Campbell Festival of Myth, Folklore and Story. This festival celebrates myth, fairy tales, good stories, poems, dance and song, and is so enjoyable that families come to it from miles around.

Such events encourage people to become more creative in their everyday lives: to try storytelling with their children, go to movement classes, nurture their creative spark. And as children learn from their parents, spark is important. Remember Roald Dahl's Danny who said that, 'My father, without the slightest doubt was the most marvellous and exciting father any boy ever had.' Danny suggests to the children reading the book that, 'When you grow up and have children of your own, do please remember something important: a stodgy parent is no fun at all. What a child wants and deserves is a parent who is *sparky*.'

Teachers and schools also need to be sparky! Schools are challenged by students who increasingly do not respond well to traditional teaching methods. Visionary teachers want to provide learning pathways for students that engage the will, activate creativity and which offer *experiential learning* rather than sedentary classroom forms of learning.

For example, in Stroud, Gloucestershire, the pioneering Ruskin Mill Further Education Course has been so successful in engaging maladjusted 16/17-year-olds in a practical, arts, crafts and environmentally based curriculum that parents are asking for this active approach to education for their 'normal' teenagers! So a Waldorf College is to be established in Autumn 2000 using the whole community as a learning environment, with students negotiating their own curriculum with a foundation of core learning activities.

So how do TV and the VDU/cathode ray screen media affect children?

Some helpful information on how the electronic media affect young children's senses will be presented. These media are here to stay, and both parents and school need to make their own free decisions on media use.

Firstly, every child is affected by TV in different ways, depending on their personality, their temperament, constitution and age. The younger the child, the more susceptible and less able to make choices about switching off. Some active children just walk away from the TV! Others are caught at once.

Here I will concentrate on the effect of TV watching, regardless of content on the development of the senses and nervous systems of young children.

William Wordsworth wrote of his experience when as a boy:

There was a time when meadow grove and stream,
The earth, and every common sight,
To me did seem apparelled in celestial light,
The glory and the freshness of a dream.

On growing older, the poet observed: 'The things which I have seen I now can see no more;' The youth who perceives 'the vision splendid... [of nature]... at length, [as a] man, perceives it die away, And fade into the light of common day.'

When we consider the openness of babies and infants to all that happens, to their powers of absorption and selfless imitation, we can appreciate the vital part played by their senses. Just as food nourishes the physical organism, so the experiences of touch, warmth, movement, sight, sound, taste, smell and well-being bring the world to the attention of the child. The exercise of the senses also nourishes the central nervous system and the brain, which enables the developing child to wake up into the world around her.

When children are brought up in an environment where their senses cannot develop in a healthy way, they do not thrive, as for example in orphans. Children who are cuddled, played with, conversed with and who experience a stimulating home life are more likely to thrive.

Our sensory experiences support our ideas, feeling and actions, even our sense of identity. This was shown dramatically in experiments with volunteers undergoing 'sensory deprivation' conditions, as a preparation for manned space flights in the United States. People floated motionless in water at blood heat, in total silence, wearing goggles that totally excluded light, and gloves which reduced the sense of touch. Initially, many volunteers fell asleep. On waking, some experienced hallucinations, fantasies, dreams, and distorted impressions of their bodies, as, for example, their arms or legs growing and floating away. Such experiments demonstrated how vital normal sensory experience is to maintain a balanced state of mind.

Given the importance of healthy sense experience for our normal functioning, and the far more vivid nature of children's sense experience, what effects does television-watching have on sensory development?

When watching television, a young child may be in a darkened room – the light of day is screened out. He is motionless, which is an uncharacteristic state for a child whose natural condition is one of continual play activity and movement. (An athlete reputed to have imitated all the actions of a two-year-old was exhausted in a short time – the child, however, was still as fresh as a daisy.) Whilst watching television the child is sitting down, the eyes are fixed, hardly move and are slightly defocused.

The senses used to watch television are sight and hearing. The other senses are largely unnecessary. Children who are playing and active will have more opportunities to develop their senses than children spending the same time watching television. 'Television' children may find it harder to 'come to their senses' having been deprived of a rich sensory diet.

A common reaction of someone discovering that my own children rarely watched television was, 'What do you *do* instead? What do you *watch?* Aren't you depriving them of so many experiences?'

They did not understand that television is a *second-hand* experience. I believe that for children an ounce of real experience is worth a ton of second-hand experience! This point was well made in a cartoon showing a child watching a sunset on television, whilst exactly the same sunset could be seen through the window. Or a mother switching off the computer, inviting her child to go and join the great interactive game of life.

To nourish the development of young children's senses is simple. They need to touch and feel the textures around them. Infants go through a stage of 'playing with their food'. By imitating the activities of adults, such as sweeping, baking, gardening and tidying, infants discover the everyday world. All the varied activities in home and garden, at the seaside, of building things, of playing games such as 'mums and dads', 'hospitals' or 'trains' – all call on the senses.

Children deprived of rich sensory experiences need to have play therapy in the nursery school. Teachers may have to put such children through a crash 'course' of such activities as water play, sand play, feeling things and mixing dough. This phenomenon of the 'play-deprived child' has been observed by many nursery teachers. They say that play-deprivation is not primarily connected with a child's socio-economic background, but rather with the amount of television-watching in the family.

Whilst many people may concede that excessive television-watching can deprive children of more healthy sense experiences, they may not readily agree that television-watching is sensory deprivation. However, this was demonstrated dramatically by psychologists Fred and Merrelyn Emery, who compared brain-wave patterns of television viewers to those undergoing lengthy sensory deprivation. The brainwave patterns on the electro-encephalograph showed that a person watching television for a few minutes was as seriously affected as someone subjected to a period of ninety-six hours sensory deprivation.

The twelve senses

Traditionally, there were five senses attributed to the human being, plus a 'sixth' sense added by hearsay. Physiologists have included a few more, such as the senses of balance and of movement, whilst several 'social senses' such as the 'sense of identity', or a 'sense of language and meaning' have been suggested. Each sense provides us with a window on the world, and we experience reality through a 'circle' of such windows as we pay more attention to one sense and then another.

The more bodily senses give us an immediate experience of our organism. Balance enables us to experience our bodies in space; touch sketches the boundary of our skin; the sense of life tells us how we are feeling – whether we are well or out of sorts, and the sense of movement brings the perception of the motions of the body's muscles, limbs or joints. Balance, touch, movement and well-being involve us deeply in our own bodily experiences – we trust what these senses tell us.

The senses of taste and smell enable us to find out about substances outside our bodies – in very personal ways since each person develops her own 'sense of taste'. With sight we perceive colours, light and shade in our surroundings. For many people, 'seeing is believing', although more doubting people, like St. Thomas, may rely on their sense of touch for conclusive information. Another sense, the sense of warmth, tells us about relationships between warmer and colder things in the environment – about whether we ourselves are gaining or losing warmth from the surroundings.

Whilst sight and warmth take us into the environment, the sense of hearing enables us to penetrate into the heart of things. The tone of a bell informs us about the quality of such materials from which it is made. The eyes may be deceived in trying to discover the material of which an object is made, but if it produces a sound, any deception is uncovered and we recognise if it is made of plastic, metal or wood.

Since the sense of hearing enables us to communicate with other people, it is above all a social sense. It is complemented by other 'social senses' which, whilst difficult to pin down physiologically, yet are essential if a person is to participate in social life. There is the sense of word, which enables us to perceive the gestures, movements and patterns which are shaped by a speaker into a stream of sounds. This sense gives us a 'feeling for language', and even if we do not understand what is being said we recognise that it 'makes sense' and is not gibberish.

Lastly, there is a subtle sense of 'feel' for the other as a person, as an identity, which can be experienced when 'making contact' with someone. These latter three senses of hearing, of word and of the sense of the 'I' of another person are very dependent on social life for their development and conversely without these there is no social life to develop them.

In the course of growing up through school, the different senses need to be nurtured more strongly according to the children's stages of development. Many activities in play groups and Kindergartens are usually practical – such as household tasks, cooking, constructing things, simple arts and crafts. Materials, substances, playthings and an environment of a sound kind have a positive influence, since it is through the senses that the world around is taken up into the child's experience – hence the importance of first-hand experiences with honest materials. Such an early environment creates security of trust in the world, for life. If children experience materials or objects which are a kind of lie – removed from real first-hand experience – then this produces an insecurity in the child, especially in trusting what the senses bring to him.

In the primary and middle schools, children need to be exercised artistically if their senses are to be fully developed. Through painting, which is of crucial importance to children, the world of colour, movement and warmth becomes a central experience for them. Music, language, art and poetry exercise the finer senses, whilst modelling or crafts enliven particularly the 'will' senses of movement, touch and balance. For it is artistic activities which awaken and develop the senses in a healthy way.

Children need to experience the beauty of the world.

At secondary level, when teenagers become much more able to perceive in a detached way, science may help the capacity for accurate, objective observation to develop. The arts – especially if used in a social way as in modern drama teaching – may be of real help in exploring relationships and in awakening the social senses. Above all, teenagers need the experience that 'the world is true'.

Television's effects on the senses

Young children, in the process of discovering the world, are faced with the problem of 'sensing' if television pictures are 'real' or not, if there is in fact a man in the box or if the screen is a window on a different world. Reports of certain primitive people's responses to cinema films – of being very concerned about where the actor has gone once he leaves the screen – demonstrate the initial confusion technology has on unsophisticated adults. From this we can envisage how puzzling television must be to children who are just becoming aware of the differences and variety of sensory experience. My three-year-old son asked, 'Is there really an orchestra in the box?' or 'Is that man really dead?'

Television is a deceptive medium to place in reach of children as they are learning to find their way in the everyday world and are developing a general 'sense' of its reality. Think of the contrast between live puppets and a show produced on the TV screen. The live performance holds children spellbound, they can see the puppets and can enter the 'make-believe' world of the story in a complete and uncontradictory way. But television puts over a vast number of images, people, and happenings that are second-hand reproductions of things taking place at a distance. Furthermore many events happening on the screen – the technical tricks, the cartoon antics, all the artificial unusualness used to attract the viewer – cannot take place in real life.

So young children are faced with a 'real world' which they need to get used to through the normal development of the senses, and a television world where events happen which are unknown and often impossible in everyday life.

A mother described an incident with her five-year-old stepdaughter who is a tele-addict:

About six months ago she ran into the road and was hit by a car, and fortunately escaped with one bruise and shock. A few hours after the accident she asked me what had happened and I explained, telling her that she was a very lucky girl. I asked, 'What would have happened if you had fallen under the wheels?' and she answered, 'I'd jump up again like the Pink Panther!'

One father, on taking his young son to the zoo was so disturbed by such comments as 'I've already seen all this on television!' that he got rid of television altogether. Reality, he concluded, cannot compete with a box which shows close-ups of tigers, lions and rhinos, scenes which one never meets in ordinary life in such rapid succession. He also felt that television was dulling his child's sense of wonder.

Television and sight

Television affects our sense of sight. Its organ, the eye, responds to colour, light and darkness on the one hand and movement on the other. In fact, movement and balance – two other distinct senses – are intimately connected with the eye. One's eye is in continual movement, busy gauging distance, height and depth which are the essential elements of perspective. The eyes are perpetually fixing objects in their vision, accommodating and shifting their focus. It takes time to learn how to perceive objects, for example, a two-year-old will recognise again a triangle that has been rotated 120 degrees, only after rotating his head also – visual exploration is therefore a prerequisite of seeing.

In adults, perception is dependent on all kinds of exploratory eye movements, from consciously directed ones to involuntary small ones which shift the image over the fovea when the eye seems fixated on a motionless object. Interestingly, in the context of television's effects on the eye, when such scanning motions are artificially suppressed, the image breaks up into fragments. We need to 'finger over the visual field with our gaze' as one physiologist observed.

Constant eye movement is required for a healthy eye. Lack of eye movement may be a symptom of ageing, and eye specialists can give exercises to help older people keep their eyes 'young'.

For focusing we need conscious attention, vigilance and concentration; in short, we have to exert ourselves to co-operate with the faculties this sense provides for us.

Attention is needed for good observation and focalisation. William James wrote that 'everyone knows what attention is... Focalisation, concentration of consciousness are of its essence. It is a condition which has a real opposite in the confused, dazed, "scatterbrained state" which in French is called distraction'. Such attention requires effort and cannot be 'sustained for more than a few seconds at a time'.

Television-watching is a visually passive activity. One's head is stationary, the eyes are practically motionless and do not continually move to get 'fixes' on objects as for normal sight, and they are slightly 'defocused' to take in the whole screen. The accent is on peripheral vision rather than on central vision which is active in the state of attention described above. Another effect is that, whilst watching television one's eye muscles are not being exercised and one's vigilance is decreased through the necessary defocusing of the eyes. There is little need for accommodating eye movement – or rather, this is kept at a constant level to make up for the nature of television which is a slightly blurred, low definition medium (compared with the clearer image of cinema films, for example). Some ophthalmologists recommend TV viewing for post-operative eye patients, just to keep the eyes stilled.

Apart from affecting the eye's mechanics in such a drastic fashion, television affects people's attention. The Emerys maintain that television both 'destroys the capacity of the viewer to attend' and also 'by taking over a complex of direct and indirect neural pathways, decreases vigilance'. They say that the television-watching state of mind is a form of distraction, as opposed to concentration and focalisation.

Furthermore, the Emerys write that in spite of the high volume of content coming from the television, the mechanics of eye and brain receive this input as if it were a simple visual stimulus. Television is therefore an impoverished sensory environment.

The foregoing arguments may lead to the conclusion that television affects children's vigilance, attention and concentration adversely.

So far we have been discussing effects applying specifically to the mature senses of adults. But how does television affect babies' and toddlers' developing sense of sight?

The perceptual world is not a finished product which is the same for everyone, but it is shaped according to a person's age. Children's experiences happen in a vivid world in which things are attractive and repulsive before they focus into abstract qualities like squareness or blackness. Piaget showed how optical illusions decrease with age, and how children's perception of space develops. For the first few months objects do not 'exist' if they are not moving or doing something. Holding or manipulating an object gives it reality, and when it disappears, it is gone for good. Space, like 'mouth space' or 'grasping space', is separate and related to activity.

At the eighth to tenth month, the object is seen to be more

independent. Piaget offered a watch to a nine-month-old who played with it. When it was hidden under a pillow, the baby fetched it. Even though the baby saw the watch being hidden in a different place the second time he still looked in the first hiding place.

At about sixteen months, the toddler perceives the object as having permanence independent of himself. Space becomes a field in which things happen, as opposed to being bound up with activity. Perhaps the game of 'peek-a-boo' is a way for babies and toddlers to get used to seeing loved ones come and go, yet still feeling they are 'there'.

The sense of sight continues to develop, and it is only at around the age of eleven to twelve that the sense for perspective emerges. From the standpoint of perceptual development, therefore, television may seriously harm the acquiring of such concepts as space by infants. Furthermore, the two-dimensional screen inhibits the development of a sense of depth and perspective.

Listening and observing

Kindergarten teachers are saying they have to teach children to listen. Although most children love stories, their attention span seems shorter and a minority find it hard to listen at all. But as soon as such children begin to make their own inner gesture-like 'pictures' of the story, they are able to listen; however, teachers comment on how much *better* story-tellers they need to be nowadays to hold children's attention.

Presumably, the background sound of radio, cassette or television at home is so prevalent that the sense of hearing is dulled. Since television is more visual than aural, and unless adults converse with children and tell them stories, children's sense of hearing is not being fully exercised. One piece of research showed that 25 years ago the average person could distinguish between 300,000 sounds; now it is only 180,000, reflecting an ongoing decrease in the brain's sensitivity.

Observational skills may also not be developed by viewing – hence the need to help children *see* flowers, animals, and birds. Many infant, Kindergarten and junior teachers I know have observed a 'withdrawal' from the senses in moderate and heavy-viewing children. They therefore need to teach therapeutically to cultivate the ability to 'see a world in a grain of sand'.

Movement and balance

Some older teachers can still distinguish the 'viewers' from 'non-viewers' in a class, by their posture, limb control and how they sit. Audrey McAllen, a special education advisor, wrote on movement and television:

After many years of working with children who have learning difficulties one sees clearly how unconnected the present-day child is with the interaction of hands and limbs. They do not bother to lift their legs high enough to throw a ball under them, the hand collides with the thigh. Also the left leg seems heavier than the right and harder for them to lift. When classes have been screened for learning problems, this symptom of limb heaviness is now general among children.

And you can experience this 'limb heaviness' for yourself after watching TV. Perhaps this is why there are currently so many popular types of movement class for adults such as Tai Chi or yoga: to counteract the effects of computer work and our sedentary lifestyle, for example,

The movement sense gives us the feeling of having a reason to be here, a sense of purpose developed from wanting to go from one place to another. This sense enables us, through our muscles to perceive if we are still or moving, and where our body is in space. Young children subtly imitate the movements in their environment, resonating, for example, to electronic movements. Learning to walk, to develop dexterity and co-ordination all relate to the movement sense.

So cramping movement through TV and computers can have disruptive affects: consider hyperactivity, attention deficit disorder, and forms of dyslexia when letters move up and down in the visual field. Dr Harry Levinson treats certain forms of dyslexia and hyperactivity with travel sickness pills. These children, he thinks, suffer from a kind of 'motion sickness'. Certain children's ability to read increases remarkably after taking these pills, because the disturbed sense of movement is calmed down.

Alan Hall, a physicist investigating electromagnetic fields, noticed the effects of rapidly oscillating, low level electromagnetic fields coming from computers and TVs: 'When one comes within two feet or 18 inches, one can feel the muscles tighten up slightly, and over time a feeling of "electrostress".' So think how such subtle oscillations can effect balance and movement in young children, going from your own direct experience, he suggests.

Balance is also affected by TV watching. And how many times do adults say they want to find balance in their lives! Balance is centred in the inner ear, sensing the pull of the earth, it gives us a sense of uprightness. It gives us a bodily, grounded reference point, a feeling of inner calm and security in space. So think of the modern dizzy pace of life and how this can knock us off balance!

Achieving balance is a major achievement for infants, as well as that of standing upright, free to start moving as an independent being in the world. Cheryl Sanders stresses that balance disorders, resulting from things like viewing, can have devastating affects on children: 'The disruption of balance causes a certain sinking feeling in the stomach, a dizziness that might be familiar to spinning about 10 or twelve times, then trying to walk straight. Imagine if this feeling were present every time you wanted to read, or write. What if the feeling were more subtle, so that you could not figure out what it was, but you knew you were feeling awful when at school, especially in some classes, but not in others like art or music... and what if lack of co-ordination was extended to any attempt to participate in games, or even just trying to run across the playground without being laughed at?'

Television closes down the human nervous system

The Emerys propose that 'television as a simple, constant, repetitive and ambiguous visual stimulus gradually closes down the nervous system of man'. In an adult's brain the left and right hemispheres have distinct, specialised functions. Each hemisphere governs the activities of the opposite side of the body. The right hemisphere, for instance, controls the movements of your left hand.

The 'critical' left brain can process one stimulus at a time. This leads to orderly thought sequences, linear thinking, analysis, distinguishing parts. The verbal and logical functions are important. The right brain can process whole clusters of stimuli at once, leading to a grasp of a complex wholes – such as a face. The processes of thinking in images and pictures are important. As mentioned previously, viewing tunes out the left brain. According to the Emerys, in adults subjected to electro-encephalographs, whilst watching television, the left hemisphere is hardly active at all, registering a minimal holding pattern. They suggest that 'viewing is at the conscious level of somnambulism'. The right hemisphere does register the television images, although since the cross-referencing of our subconscious intelligence between left and right has been 'knocked out', these cannot easily be brought to consciousness. Hence the difficulty most people have in recalling much information from a programme.

Other researchers into brainwave patterns whilst watching television confirm the Emerys' findings. Dr Eric Pepper is a Professor of Interdisciplinary Sciences at San Francisco State University. He claims '...that the alpha wave patterns which rapidly become dominant whilst watching are a sign of being in a totally passive condition and being unaware of the world outside of the pictures which one is seeing.' The right phrase for alpha patterns is really 'spaced-out'. Not orienting. 'When someone pays attention to something external, such alpha patterns disappear.'

Babies have unspecialized brains. Indeed, it is only at about twelve that the left and right sides are fully specialised. Babies seem to have some sort of 'non-verbal thought': for example, they recognise human faces.

In the second year, toddlers learn to speak, and language comes to the fore. At this time each brain hemisphere is apparently equally mature; lesions on the left side are no more harmful to language development than on the right side, and vice versa. Similar lesions in the left hemispheres of adults might cause significant linguistic problems.

As language develops, the brain specialises into the two hemispheres of verbal and or non-verbal thinking. Learning increasingly comes from verbal activities.

However, television in the early years when the brain is so malleable and sensitive, prolongs the dominance of the non-verbal 'right hemisphere' functions. The trance-like state of many child viewers, especially if induced for 20-30 hours per week, may seriously inhibit the development of the verbal-logical 'left hemisphere' activities.

Furthermore, children exposed to television – a medium which prolongs the dominance of non-verbal 'right' hemisphere activities – may not take full advantage of the special 'language sensitive' period of influence. Just as there are 'tides in the affairs of men' so there are tides of 'readiness' in the child's development, for example, language readiness. If a child does not learn to speak during this period of readiness, it may be hard for her to make up for this deficiency later on.

Health visitors and speech therapists are concerned about the increasing numbers of young children who can hardly speak. What appear to be speech impairments, are in fact children who have had little family conversation, no nursery rhymes, and whose parents prefer dummies (pacifiers) and television.

When neurologists such as Dr Eric Pepper assert that 'television trains people only for being zombies' – it may be time to ask: 'Do we want this state of consciousness to be induced in our children?'

To conclude, viewing at an early age may hinder the development of the senses, such as light, hearing, balance, movement – and, indeed, offers us a poor sensory diet. Over-stimulated, children may 'withdraw from their senses', and need therapeutic exercises. The patterning the brain needs for language development is hindered by viewing.

However, given the extensive research on the effects of viewing on young children, it is up to parents and school to make up their own minds. And at a time when there are so many creative alternatives, families are voting with their feet! However, schools are challenged as well to put more spark into learning. I remember a Waldorf colleague answering a parent asking him about whether she should be concerned about her child's viewing: 'Over the next few months, your daughter will grow out of most of her viewing, as she gets involved in all the creative work we do!' In other words, a lively family and school life is enough to get children 'out of the box'.

Martin Large lectured in management and behavioural science for many years in higher education. He works as a facilitator in participative planning, community building, and learning. He is the author of *Who's Bringing Them Up?*

Contact:

Hawthorn Press,
Hawthorn House,
1 Lansdown Lane,
Stroud,
Glos. GL5 1BJ

Tel: (01453) 757040
Fax: (01453) 751138
E-mail: mhclarge@aol.com

References

Fred and Merrelyn Emery, *A Choice of Futures – To Enlighten or Inform* No.ACP 2600 1975, Centre for Continuing Education, Australian National University.

Jane M. Healey, *Endangered Minds* Touchstone, New York, 1990.

Martin Large, *Who's Bringing Them Up? How to kick the T.V. habit* Hawthorn Press, Stroud, Second edition 1992.

H. N. Levinson, M.D., *A Scientific Watergate, Dyslexia* Stonebridge Publishing Ltd, Lake Success, New York 1994.

Thomas Moore, *The Re-Enchantment of Everyday Life* Hodder, London 1996.

Cheryll Sanders, in the Foreword to *Games Children Play* Kim Brooking-Payne, Hawthorn Press, Stroud, UK 1996.

A. Soesman, *The Twelve Senses* Hawthorn Press, Stroud 1996.

9. Moving from an ad hoc to a national strategic approach to addressing racism in the early years in Britain

Jane Lane

I believe that all children have a right to fairness and justice. By this I mean that they should be entitled, as of right, as their due, to have equality of access, opportunity and treatment in everything that will enable them to maximise their potential and minimise their exclusion in their early childhood and later. Most people will agree with this. It is more than a legal right – many people believe that it is also a moral right. But people in different countries may have differing concepts of the term 'right' and of 'moral' and even of the definition of a 'child'.

The whole concept of 'rights' is philosophically, socially and politically contentious. In Britain the concept is under-developed. Instead the discussion has mainly been around the concept of equality. In practice this concept has suited our purpose as it is measurable – we can, generally, measure equality of access, opportunity and treatment. Whereas the concept of rights is abstract, that of equality is concrete. In other words the issue is policy-orientated aimed, in terms of work with young children, at provision and attitudes.

Of course, not all children are born with equal potential, but this does not impair their right to equality of access, opportunity and treatment – their right to fairness and justice.

To compound this individual inequality many societies, both historically and in the present, are unequal. The histories of slavery (largely worldwide though manifested in differing forms), antisemitism, anti-Traveller / Roma / Gypsy persecution, western European colonialism and imperialism have resulted in many societies being structured on racism.

Similarly, though for different reasons, sexism and homophobia are embedded and endemic in most societies. And disabled people are often marginalised, ignored and sometimes ridiculed.

People are often judged by what work they do, how much money they have, where they live, what they wear, what they look like, the way they speak and on many other grounds. Social class divisions in many societies are alive and well.

To summarise, in most societies some individual children and some groups of children start off their lives disadvantaged and frequently discriminated against. Inequality is endemic and usually institutionalised. This does not mean that everyone is personally prejudiced or discriminates against others, although many are prejudiced and do discriminate. But the institutions themselves, and their practices and procedures, have the effect of disadvantaging and discriminating against groups of people, including children. Such a society is Britain.

My specific concern is with racial equality, the right of young children to be free of racism and what those of us working in the early years field with young children can do to address it. This chapter aims to describe the work done in Britain, focussing on England in particular. I recognise the different backgrounds and experiences from which we all come. This is just one example from one country at one moment in time. I hope it will be seen in this context.

Some real life examples

To put racism in the context of reality I will cite just two examples:

– a white grandmother, whose daughter is married to a Sikh man, very recently collected her 3 year-old granddaughter from her nursery and took her home. When her daddy came to collect her from her grandmother's he put his arms out and said 'Come and give me a hug'. The little girl recoiled and said 'You're not my daddy, you're black'. This demonstrates the power of racist attitudes even over a little girl who loves her Asian daddy.

– a four year old white girl living in the north of Scotland, where very few black people live, was visited by her aunt and a black Nigerian man friend. When she saw the black man she said 'Are you a boxer?' When he said he wasn't she said 'Well, you must have been in prison then'. This demonstrates that she had learnt these attitudes from somewhere but that it was only the reality of the presence of the black man that revealed what she was thinking. If he had not visited, her family might never have known what she had learnt.

Research and police records show that children as young as five may be perpetrators of racist abuse and harassment.[1] This was also found in the report of the Stephen Lawrence Inquiry (where Stephen Lawrence, a 18 year old black young man was stabbed to death just because he was black, by a group of white young men).[2]

Racism is profoundly dysfunctional in society.

Establishing a common basis of understanding

In order to establish a common understanding of the work being done in Britain I need to put the issues around racial equality in the early years into a context – to describe the background of this work. To clarify the issues under discussion I need to define what I am talking about and identify and explain the assumptions I make in this context.

1) Definitions:

Terminology. Terminology is constantly changing. Many people are beginning to question the use of the term 'ethnic minority' or 'minority ethnic' because of its connotations of being 'less important'. But there are so many difficulties and conflicts with any suggestions that compromises are inevitable. In this chapter I will use the terms which appear most appropriate to Britain and young children – 'black, Asian and other minority ethnic groups' as referring to people of African Caribbean origin, Asian origin (including south Asian and all other Asian countries and regions) and minority ethnic groups (including Jewish, Greek, Turkish and Irish people, Travellers/Gypsies and refugees and asylum seekers). White people also comprise many groups but while most of them do not experience racism some do – for example, Irish and Jewish people, Travellers/Gypsies and sometimes refugees and asylum seekers (those from minority ethnic groups).

Racism. I am using this term as a 'package' comprising several elements – racial prejudice, racial discrimination, racial stereo-typing, racial harassment, ethnocentrism, institutional racism and structural racism.[3]

Anyone can be racially prejudiced or discriminatory. But in Britain the full force of racism nearly always lies within the power of the majority of white people, usually white men.

2) Assumptions:

– all inequalities/equalities are equally important to the people affected – for each person or group to be discriminated against on any ground is unacceptable. I am focussing on racism here but all oppressions, all inequalities, need to be addressed integrally wherever possible.

– an understanding that racism is embedded/endemic in our society – in multiracial as well as in largely white areas – research reveals the extent of rural racism.[4] This means taking account of it in all early years services and settings.[5]

– research shows that children learn their attitudes, including their racial attitudes, at a very young age.[6] The evidence in Britain shows that white children are much more likely to be racially prejudiced than black and Asian children, although some white children may *not* be racially prejudiced and some black and Asian children *may* be racially prejudiced. And clearly there may be a whole range of attitudes from violent to mild. People often say that children don't notice colour – but this may be because adults don't talk about skin colour differences. It is a bit of a 'taboo area' like sex and death. And they can usually distinguish between a red and a yellow ball! We cannot assume that children who don't reveal their attitudes are not learning to be racially prejudiced under our very noses. Perhaps we may think young children are not learning to be prejudiced because we don't want this to be true.

– racism affects and damages all children, but in different ways. If we want to address the learning of racist attitudes and behaviour it is therefore important to work with all children in their early years on two accounts:

- to support black, Asian and other children who may experience prejudice and discrimination, to try to engender an ethos of equal value and respect, to take account of their individual and group needs and to ensure they have equal access to the full range of learning opportunities

- to help *all* children to do two specific things:
  i) to promote (or learn) positive attitudes and behaviour to differences between people and
  ii) to counter (or unlearn), if possible, any negative attitudes and behaviour that they may have already learnt – from wherever they have learnt them

  Because any children (black, Asian, white or other children) may be racially prejudiced against someone, we need to work with all children, even though the reality is that white children are *much* more likely to be deeply prejudiced and act it out in their behaviour.

– evidence of widespread racial discrimination in British society.[7] If we are to break the cycle of children learning racist attitudes and growing up to practise them, as individuals and as part of institutions, we need to take action.

What are the possible effects of racism on black, Asian, other minority ethnic, Irish, Jewish, Traveller/Gypsy and white children?

For most children subjected to racism it is hurtful and may interfere with their ability to learn. It may damage their concept of self identity. It can affect their behaviour, their motivation and their confidence. They need to learn that racism is not their fault and is not the result of anything they have done.

Racism also damages white children. It may lead them to believe that black, Asian and other people who experience racism are somehow less human than they are. It may blunt their sensitivity to others and reinforce false notions of their own superiority. It may reinforce their perceptions of reality by failing to provide them with the full range of information on which they can make their own judgements. It may prevent them from learning concepts of empathy to others – concepts that are fundamental to respecting and valuing one another.

Discussing racism

Racism is often an uncomfortable topic to discuss. If we are to counter it in individuals and in institutions we need to do it sensitively and in a non-threatening way. No-one changes their attitudes or behaviour under threat or being made to feel guilty. We need to adopt a no-blame culture where mutual trust is established and where recognition is given to people's own experiences and possible feelings of disadvantage and disempowerment in society.

The history of addressing racism in the early years in Britain

In the sixties the issue of learning English as an additional language was seen as a priority. Later on there was a perceived need for black and Asian children's cultures to be included and valued. This was called multiculturalism. It was largely seen as being applicable only in multiracial areas. White children's cultures (however they could be described) were seldom included. The failure to recognise or accept that cultures in a racist society are ranked in a racial hierarchy led many black and Asian families to object to what they saw as marginalising their children and not giving them equal access to the full range of learning opportunities.

In the seventies and eighties there was a great improvement in the availability of appropriate resources for young children reflecting the multiracial, multicultural, multilingual and multifaith society. Services and settings often developed equal opportunity policies but mostly just about employment. However two pieces of legislation contributed positively to addressing practical issues – the 1976 Race Relations Act (making racial discrimination in employment and services unlawful) and the 1989 Children Act (requiring registration and inspection procedures for early years provision to address racial equality and talking about the rights of children to 'freedom from discrimination such as racism').

Several critically important organisations were set up in this time. They lobbied for appropriate resources (including books, dolls, posters, jigsaws) and challenged negative ones – and set up groups reflecting the specific needs and interests of black and Asian communities. They set up training courses about racism for tutors and lecturers in childcare/education Their on-going contributions to raising the issue of racism nationally has been crucial.[8]

In the nineties training for childcare/education in the voluntary sector and in further education courses began to address racism as integral within a formalised programme and some good work was done. In higher education / teacher education courses, for various reasons (largely to do with their national organisational arrangements) there was much less work done. Indeed the curriculum for formal teacher education devised by the Teacher Training Agency (TTA) failed to acknowledge the inequalities embedded in our society at all. Student teachers were thus ill-prepared for teaching in multiracial Britain. The curriculum objectives (under the Qualifications and Curriculum Authority {QCA}) and inspection regulations (under the Office for Standards in Education {OFSTED}) made passing reference to issues of culture but little more.

But overall it was very difficult to address racial equality effectively because of the huge diversity in the organisation of the early years – in inspections, registration, the curriculum, qualifications, training, employment conditions and pay, the cost of a child's place, in the variety of settings themselves and who was responsible for them. This was often referred to as the 'Under Fives Muddle'. And, crucially, there was no national government (or its agencies) commitment either to recognise the endemic racism in society or to support those trying to implement racial equality in the early years. Indeed the 'muddle' itself was often seen as contributing to diversity and maximising choice. This ad hoc approach made it virtually impossible to address racism comprehensively and strategically. Furthermore, in the eighties in particular, there were frequent media 'witch-hunts' against anyone trying to address racism in education.

Recent changes in the organisation of the early years

The Labour government, elected in 1997, began to rationalise this muddled situation. It set up integrated early years services and early years development and childcare partnerships (EYDCPs) in every local authority, each required to produce a Plan of its proposed activities in line with specific Guidance. It established curriculum guidance for the Foundation stage of a child's education and is in the process of setting up model early years 'centres of excellence' throughout the country. It has not yet finalised its arrangements for unifying inspection and regulation of early years settings. So, for the first time, given this new structure and framework, it became possible to address racism comprehensively and strategically. Getting rid of racism is very unlikely to happen by chance or by goodwill alone – there needs to be a plan.

Recent action by government and others to promote racial equality and address racism in the early years

At its election the present government gave a strong commitment to equality of access and opportunity. In putting this into practice it has been gradually building up a programme that requires and encourages everyone in the early years field to address inequality generally. It has focussed on an inclusive society.

Department of Education and Employment (DfEE) Guidance to EYDCPs with regard to writing their Plans for the early years has, over the last three years, required increasingly more detailed action to address equal opportunities to be taken. It has listed specific criteria for this including:

– a policy statement

– an implementation programme covering what is to be done, by whom and within what timescale, the roles and responsibilities of everyone, an analysis of which children face access obstacles to services, how to ensure that everyone has equal access to provision aiming to reflect the profile of the local population

– a monitoring mechanism to evaluate the implementation and effectiveness of the policy

– how the EYDCP has consulted with families of all groups

– details of training of staff on equal opportunity issues and implementation of the Plan

The specific groups of children mentioned cover: minority ethnic groups, different genders and ages, refugees, those with disabilities or learning difficulties/special educational needs, those who are 'homeless' or 'in care' and those learning English. In the next Guidance we hope to see Travellers/Gypsies, asylum seekers, those with a religion or belief and those from various social and family structures/ backgrounds also included.

The DfEE in its 1998 Guidance for EYDCPs highlighted the Early Years Trainers Anti Racist Network (EYTARN) publication

'Planning for Excellence', containing a 'Framework for Equality' and sent a copy to every local authority in England.[9] It also requires all bids for approval to be early excellence centres to have equality policies in line with this framework.

The TTA, responsible for teacher recruitment and the curriculum in institutions providing teacher education, has recently published guidance/resource materials for institutions on raising the attainment of minority ethnic pupils.[10] Unfortunately its suggestions for issues to be addressed are not mandatory.

The new curriculum guidance for the Foundation stage of children's learning is a huge improvement on previous documents and refers to ethnicity, culture, religion, home language, mutual respect, celebrating and acknowledging differences and positive resources.[11]

The DfEE draft consultative documents on national standards for the regulation of day care by OFSTED have stronger statements on equality of opportunity than previously and provide a potentially useful framework for addressing the issues for those who are committed to address them.[12]

In February 1999 the report of the Stephen Lawrence Inquiry was published with massive attendant publicity. In many senses this was a watershed. Apart from the fact that it demonstrated the existence and force of institutional racism to all, it brought sharply to the fore the facts of the pain of racism for its recipients. The text stressed the importance of ensuring that 'the minds of present and future generations are not allowed to become violent and maliciously prejudiced' and 'the need for education and example at the youngest age'. This report has been of critical importance in raising the issue of racism more than ever before with everyone working in the early years, including policy makers and those training/educating people to work with children.

The Early Years Trainers Anti Racist Network's
'Framework for Equality'

The 'Framework for Equality' cited above has been seminal in suggesting a strategic way of working for EYDCPs and in influencing government. It consists of six non-hierarchical components each with a list of action points covering the roles and responsibilities of partnerships, early years services and settings, anti-discriminatory legislation and policy making. All these reflect the principles identified above –

* to support black, Asian and other children who may experience prejudice and discrimination, to try to engender an ethos of equal value and respect, to take account of their individual and group needs and to ensure they have equal access to the full range of learning opportunities

* to help *all* children to do two specific things:
  i) to promote (or learn) positive attitudes and behaviour to differences between people and
  ii) to counter (or unlearn), if possible, any negative attitudes and behaviour that they may have already learnt – from wherever they have learnt them

This framework approach involves everyone in working towards the same objective of equality for all and offers important benefits – establishing links between people, sharing information and identifying responsibilities and roles. But, crucially, it ensures that all aspects of the service are addressed, every decision and activity is assessed for its implications for equality. A key issue is who is appointed to work in the early years. The most important is having a commitment to implement equality in practice – we believe this is measurable in the selection process – from which the skills, understanding and knowledge of how to put the commitment into practice can be developed. Some of the important issues raised in the six components are listed below:

1) **Partnerships** – have responsibility for ensuring equality is implemented throughout the service and settings by devising a policy statement, implementation programme and monitoring mechanism, consulting with black, Asian and minority ethnic group families, identifying training and support needs and establishing a data base and evaluation process on all aspects of the service and settings.

2) **Early years service** – responsible for ensuring that the Partnership policy is implemented and evaluated. Collecting and analysing ethnic data and other relevant information demonstrates whether all children, of whatever ethnicity, are getting equality of access, opportunity and treatment in their early years settings. Data should also be used to examine equality in employment, an important aspect for children to see a range of people as being valuable in their lives.

3) **Policy for equality in early year settings**, including a policy on name-calling/harassment – staff, children, families/carers, community members and governors/managers/committee members are all stakeholders in the setting.[13] The process of developing a policy involving them all is critically important in facilitating their 'ownership' of it. Families/carers are very important as they play a particular role in the attitude development of their children.

4) **Antidiscriminatory legislation** – people need to be familiar with the 1975 Sex Discrimination Act, 1976 Race Relations Act and 1995 Disability Discrimination Act particularly in employment and admissions to settings.[14] Other forms of discrimination not covered by legislation need to be identified and addressed, for example, child to child name-calling/harassment.

The last two components cover the settings themselves.

5) Treating everyone with equal concern – ensuring equal value and respect for all children free of stereotypes and assumptions, ensuring equal access and entitlement to the curriculum (both overt and covert – all aspects of the development of learning skills), examining resources, valuing all languages/dialects, skin colours, physical features and implementing both multicultural and antiracist practices and procedures. This is because in a racist society cultures are ranked in a racist hierarchy.

6) Developing specific strategies with children to promote the learning of positive attitudes and behaviour to differences between people and to counter the learning of negative attitudes and behaviour that they may have already learnt – this requires sensitivity, knowledge, skills and understanding, working with families/carers to provide regular discussion about issues of concern, to encourage children to be critically aware of the world around them and to be able to develop concepts of empathy with others so that they can make up their own minds about what is fair and just. Circle time and Persona dolls (dolls and their stories used for exploring attitudes and feelings with children) are examples of this strategic approach.

People have found this framework for equality approach helpful and within their grasp – it is practical, non-threatening and specific. It guides those working with young children as to what they can do in practice. It can be adapted to suit relevant circumstances. It provides a way of measuring whether equality is being put into practice. There is also a publication on inspections based on the same framework approach.[15]

But, of course, there may be barriers making it difficult to implement the framework as quickly as one might have hoped, including time and resource limitations, family or staff hostility, people only paying lip-service and lack of training and funding. Changing attitudes and behaviour takes time – it is not possible to stop the influences of our history overnight! And many people do not know what they do not know.

Conclusions

The positive improvements at government level have not just happened because of the change of government. I do not believe the same government progress would have been made without the crucial input made by individuals and organisations over more than thirty years. They have played a critical role in raising the issue of racism and its effects on young children generally and in changing the climate about the importance of working with very young children often against hostility and apathy and in an unreceptive environment.

Their on-going activities have raised the level of awareness generally and removed many of the obstacles that were formerly in place (for example, negative resources) and developed some positive procedures and practices (for example, antidiscriminatory job recruitment and some ethnic monitoring, some effective training courses and critical analyses and evaluations of organisational practice). This has impacted on the majority of early years organisations to produce a sea change in commitment – they now largely recognise and accept the importance and significance of considering equality issues in positive ways.

But despite these valued developments there is no substitute for effective national government commitment in practice. By 1997 the scene was set for action and the ground prepared for these national changes and requirements to be put into practice. And opportunities to work with government departments and its agencies began to be possible.

It needs to be said, however, that the task of building up an understanding of the issues, of keeping up the pressure on government, of the frequently changing government officers, of being constantly vigilant, of raising issues at every available opportunity (being everywhere all the time) has not been without its stresses and setbacks. Commenting on a vast range of the never decreasing government consultation documents, drawing attention to the large number of omissions and writing critical analytical documents and reports on topical issues in whatever medium possible takes its toll. It needs dogged determination never to give up. EYTARN (my organisation), for example, has just two part-time members of staff. Working against racism, as anyone in the field will know, demands a strong commitment and a skin like an elephant to survive. It is to the credit of all those in the past and present that any successes have been achieved.

At last EYTARN is being asked for advice and information from government and its agencies. Serious heed is paid to what it says and writes. It is overwhelmed with requests for training, support and for commenting on documents produced by other organisations. The rewards of this long struggle are beginning to be felt.

Finally, the monumental task of ensuring the rights of children and ensuring their equality of access, opportunity and treatment needs to be undertaken by us all, as individuals and as members of institutions.

For all those in other countries trying to get equality issues on the national agenda I wish you well and hope that you, like us, will never give up. The issue of the future of all our children and their right to be free of racism is too important to be left to chance.

Jane Lane is the Coordinator of the Early Years Trainers Anti Racist Network (EYTARN). She was formerly an education officer at the Commission for Racial Equality, a British government sponsored organisation responsible for ensuring the implementation of the 1976 Race Relations Act. She has written and spoken widely on the importance of working with young children to encourage and support them in learning positive attitudes to differences between people and countering any negative attitudes and behaviour that they may have already learnt.

Her latest publication is 'Action for racial equality in the early years: understanding the past, thinking about the present, planning for the future' (1999), available from:

The National Early Years Network,
77 Holloway Road,
London N7 8JZ
Tel: (0207) 607 9573

or from:

EYTARN,
PO Box 28,
Wallasey CH45 9NP
Tel/fax: (0151) 639 6136
E-mail: eytarn@lineone.net.

References

1. Sibbitt, R (1997) *The perpetrators of racial harassment and racial violence* Home Office

2. The Stationery Office (1999) *The Stephen Lawrence Inquiry: report of an inquiry by Sir William Macpherson of Cluny*

3. Most people will understand the terms racial prejudice, discrimination, stereotyping and harassment. **Ethnocentrism** is viewing something from a particular ethnic perspective irrespective of others. **Institutional racism** is not usually a result of deliberate, individual action. It occurs when long-established practices and procedures, which may be official or unofficial, combine with thoughtless, (often unconscious) prejudice, stereotyping and cultural assumptions to produce discrimination and less favourable/inferior treatment on grounds of skin colour, ethnicity, culture or nationality (and sometimes on language or religion/belief). While many members of the institution may believe they are not personally prejudiced or that they do not hold stereotyped attitudes, their failure to recognise or challenge forms of racism within the institution means that they are part of the institutional racism. Only those people who recognise and challenge racism can genuinely claim to be exceptions. **Structural racism** occurs when the society and the economy operate in such a way that certain ethnic groups are disproportionately disadvantaged.

4. For example – Jay, E (1992) *Keep them in Birmingham* Commission for Racial Equality

5. I use the term 'early years services' to cover all the organisational arrangements for young children and 'early years settings' to include all provision for young children, wherever they are cared for and educated.

6. Milner, D. (1983) *Children and race: 10 years on* Ward Lock, London.
Sibbitt, R (1997) *The perpetrators of racial harassment and racial violence* Home Office Research Study 176.

Lane, J. (1999) *Action for racial equality in the early years: understanding the past, thinking about the present, planning for the future* Notes 6, p.68. National Early Years Network, London.

7. Commission for Racial Equality *Factsheets*

8. The Black Childcare Network (c/o Hearsay, 17 Brownhill Road, London SE6 2EG. Tel: 0208 697 2152).
    The Working Group Against Racism in Children's Resources (460 Wandsworth Road, London SW8 3LK. Tel: 0207 627 4594).
    The Early Years Trainers Anti Racist Network (PO Box 28 Wallasey CH45 9NP. Tel/fax: 0151 639 6136).
    The REU (formerly Race Equality Network, Unit 27/28 Angel Gate, City Road, London EC1V 2PT. Tel: 0207 278 2331).
    The Anti Racist Teacher Education Network (c/o Alison Hatt, Flat 5, 19 Hillbury Road, London SW17 8JT).
    The Centre for Young Children's Rights (356 Holloway Road, London N7 6PA. Tel: 0207 700 8127).

9. Early Years Trainers Anti Racist Network (1998) *Planning for Excellence: implementing the DfEE Guidance requirement for the equal opportunity strategy in Early Years Development Plans*

10. Teacher Training Agency (2000) *Raising the Attainment of Minority Ethnic Pupils: guidance and resource materials for providers of initial teacher training*

11. Qualifications and Curriculum Authority (2000) *Curriculum guidance for the foundation stage*

12. Department for Education and Employment (2000) *National Standards for the Regulation of Day Care* – consultation pack.

13. Early Years Trainers Anti Racist Network (2000) *Equality in Action : developing a policy for equality in early years settings* – to be published mid-November

14. Commission for Racial Equality (1996) *From cradle to school: a practical guide to racial equality in early childhood education and care*

15. Early Years Trainers Anti Racist Network (1999) *Inspecting for Excellence: a Guidance on inspecting for equality in early years settings*

10. 'Nothin' Special': In The Company of Children

O. Fred Donaldson, PhD

I remember bounding out the door of my uncle's farmhouse on the first day of summer, taking in undeciphered, all that lay before me. I disappeared quickly from the range of the adult world; I had only a short time to get beyond where I knew that I could be seen and called. I ran about hither and yon, as my mother would say, greeting the four horses meandering about the barnyard, Buster, the Saint Bernard bounding along with me, and the tall green rows of corn. At times like this I ran about attempting to be everywhere at once. As I recall, I did not leave with any plans or expectations, rather I encountered the day as an adventure, making do with whatever came to hand. Playing with the frogs in the farm pond, chasing the horses down the land, exploring the old caboose in the woods. I understood doing nothin'. I was as much inhabited by the farm as I inhabited the farm. Surrounded by the farm was like being tucked into a down comforter on a cold night.

Hours later I would hear the ringing of the large dinner bell that stood on a post outside the kitchen door. I wandered home for dinner stopping along the way for just one more little bit of play, until finally I found myself at the mudroom door.

'Hurry and get washed for dinner. Where have you been?'

'Nowhere.'

'Who were you with?'

'Nobody.'

'What were you doing?'

'Nothin' special.'

My mother smiled at my answers. She knew that I was somewhere, probably with someone, doing something. And I knew that she knew this too. So, what's going on? Sometimes I gave these answers because I was playing somewhere, in the hay loft, or chasing the horses. It isn't that I didn't know where I was or what I was doing. I was playing with the world.

This kind of nothing points to a notion of childhood that is too often only examined by eyes narrowed by the calculations of adulthood, which no longer feel the urge to journey and seek out who lives beyond our categories. In this sense 'nothing' describes a vacancy which discounts all else that might pass between people, where we experience a feeling of emptiness at the heart of being.

My reply of 'nothin' special' to my mother describes the presence of an absence or the nothing that is known to be there beyond categories setting me in a much wider constellation beyond our abstractions, categories, and pedagogies. This *nothin'* is characterized by a sense of wonder, surprise, and expectancy that keeps a child's eyes wide open. Nothin' here means everything. In this play I am initiated into the world, where borders between me and other creatures are places to explore, where the earth gets ground into our skin and a sense of belonging gets under our skin. Too often we fail to realize that we are in the 'nothin' special' presence of the sacred, because we are too preoccupied with tasks or because our categories seduce us into believing that childhood is just 'kid's stuff.'

Play with children and wild animals over the past 30 years has shown me that play is not a condiment to be added in order to spice up an ordinarily dull, lifeless existence. Play is not a vacation from life. Rather play is life's adventure with all its grace and grit, sacredness and ordinariness. Play is the cipher used in the encoding of an ancient, hieroglyphic code of primary importance through which we are brought home again. Like a haiku each play meeting focuses on a moment in which the sacredness of ordinary life is brought forth. In these encounters we are authenticated by each other and therein by all beings. It's not that I know more, but more deeply. The question about life's meaning vanishes, yet I can't point to it or define it. For a moment my soul breaks open, like a shaft of bright sunlight searing through expansive gray clouds leaving bright the ground around, providing a glimpse of life's possibility.

Play becomes an experience of trust and spirit, of heart and body, of life and death, and of grace and grit. The essence of being a playmate is to play my heart out. Literally my heart is at my fingertips. To put one's life into the hands of another is play. There is no hiding place. I have to be fearless. Within these moments is an extraordinary intensity that perhaps can best be described as fierce loving. It is powerful when life faces life and the compelling torque of meaning is compressed into each moment. Years of experience playing are consumed in these moments of contact when bodies are held in each other's grasp and spirits are released.

What follows are five brief encounters, direct expressions of life's play. Like *haiku* each meeting focuses on a moment in which the ordinariness of the sacred and the sacredness of the ordinary in life are brought forth.

One day I sit and cradle Erin, who is 18 months old and has Down Syndrome in my arms. Before our play session Erin's mother tells me her doctor recently told her that, 'Erin's brain is not growing. She has no intelligence.' She is disheartened as she interprets the doctor's words to mean that her daughter, 'is a nothing.' All too often such language ricochets within us increasing our fear and separation resulting in an absence of a presence.

As Erin squirms rapidly and haphazardly her body bends out over my arm. My hand cradles her head and my arm blends with her spine to support her rapid and unpredictable motions. We move together in spirals until she is close to my chest. Holding her head, I lower my face until I am close enough for Erin to nibble my beard. Our bodies become still and our eyes find each other. It is as if we lock in on each other. This is a time-space of connection during which Erin stops her rapid head bobbing and her eye motions slow to a steady gaze into my eyes. Erin provides me with the opportunity to share an epiphany, a small window of divine connection.

Paul was in my kindergarten class. He had leukemia. His doctors and his parents were afraid that rambunctious play would hasten his death. So, for six months we touched in a variety of other ways: he snuggled in my lap while I read stories; I carried him around the room on my shoulders; and, I lay down in the block area when he played with the blocks. But Paul didn't join in our roly-poly play.

One day about six months into the school year Paul came to me and asked if I would invite his parents into school for a meeting. The four of us met the following afternoon. Paul began quietly, with a sense of urgency, 'I want to play with Fred. I know that I am not going to live as long as the three of you, but I want to live my life as if I were.' His sincerity moved us. Through many tears we agreed that Paul could play with me. When he came to school the following day he was so excited and his play was so rambunctious, passionate and uncompromising that he was exhausted by the end of the morning. He stayed home and rested the following day. Because he played so hard when he came to school, Paul could only come to school every other day.

About a month later Paul died of leukemia.

On a June day I entered the enclosure to play with Nala, a 500 pound Barbary lioness. She was lying down near the entrance. I watched her and quickly knelt down about 15 feet away. She watched me intently, quickly stood, and trotted toward me. As she closed the distance between us my experience of time changed. Suddenly time sped up. I lost sight of her and the next instant I realized she was on me. She had somehow pounced on my back and enveloped me with her body. She landed her 500 pounds on me with overwhelming force and as gently as falling dew. Then time slowed down. I could feel her body and teeth not as weight but as presence. I felt each part of her separately and simultaneously. Her front legs completely surrounded me, holding me snuggly. I recall my fingers feeling the softness of the fur on her left paw that was a few inches from my face and being amazed that not only were her claws retracted but I could move the paw. There was no tension in her paw. At the same time she grasped my head in her jaws. I could feel her canine teeth holding my head firmly from the base of my skull up over my ears to my forehead.

I felt no fear, there was no pain, no cuts, no blood. I would never have believed that a lioness could be so fierce and gentle at the same time. After a few moments she released me and we stood calmly watching each other. In her embrace I experienced a quickening with the celerity and decisiveness of a lightning strike, the snugness of a tree bud, and the gentleness of a breath of spring breeze on my cheek. Never had it been so important and urgent, if I am not to fail the purpose for which I am created and gives me meaning, to remind myself to play my heart out. She reminds me to play each moment as if my life depends upon it.

Some months earlier between classes at a Head Start site a teacher called me in and asked me to help get a hummingbird out of the classroom. It had flown in during the break between morning and afternoon sessions. The staff had tried everything they could think of and nothing worked. They were afraid if the bird stayed in the room when the children arrived, besides making it impossible to quiet them, their excitement and noise might make it even more difficult to get the bird out, perhaps the stress would cause its death. I walked in with no idea of how to 'catch' a hummingbird. The staff had already tried everything I could think of. So, I stopped thinking, walked in, stopped in the middle of the room, and reached up. The hummingbird flew right into my open hand. I cupped my other hand over it and ran to the door, releasing it to the sky. It immediately flew up, hovered and darted off over the roof.

At a cancer retreat Pat asked me if I would show her some play activities that she could use with her teenage son. She said that they had played before her cancer had become so disabling. Even though Pat's body was frail and she often needed oxygen, her spirit was anxious to play. I showed her two play activities that she could do with her son while sitting in a chair or lying on a bed. Then I smiled and said that I had another idea. Her eyes sparkled. I demonstrated an *aikido* back roll that I use to give young children vestibular movement and cuddling.

I asked her if she would like to try it. 'Yes!', she exclaimed. Pat sat in my lap and we positioned her oxygen next to us so the cord was unhampered by our movement.

'One, Two, Three, GO!' She giggled with delight. 'More,' she exclaimed. Back and forth we rolled; our giggling filled the room. After a few rolls we rested quietly.

Pat had to leave the retreat early to be with her family. When she was ready to depart I went out to say goodbye. We hugged, kissed, and looked at each other in silence. Pat died less than a week later, but not before we experienced the joy and love, the touch and belonging of original play.

Coming out to play with the world may seem simple and frivolous with children, and cute with a hummingbird, but downright suicidal with a lioness. Re-discovering the capacity of play in the midst of cancer's or leukemia's anguish may seem impossible. But are these encounters so different from those I have everyday with children? I think not.

Here are five encounters, direct expressions in which I meet life, not in the categories in which we live our lives, but in sacred playgrounds in which unconditional kindness allows the ephemeral to coalesce in a tangible moment of grace – the realm of life in which we feel the contagion of authenticity deep within the heart of life. Play's kindness means that there is only one kind of life to which we all belong. In play there are no differences that make a difference. I touched Erin, Pat and the hummingbird with the same touch that Paul and the lioness used to surround me. To play, then, is an act of genuine responsibility, an act of trust in a life given in trust.

The true power of our capacity for play is not survival of the fittest, but the actual experience of being alive. Paul, Pat, Nala, Erin, and the hummingbird express the vitality, potency, pliancy and fertility of an aware being. The difficulty is that to play in such a circumstance means that we must not be afraid of life. Play is not just about courage in the face of attack or death, it is about the courage in the face of life.

The more I play the more I smile at my intimacy with the community of life that gathers me from all the remotest ends of my being, as if into the heart of a family singularly my own, and confirms for me a direction of spirit. Eric, Pat, Paul, the lioness and the hummingbird provide me with a sense of the living mystery of what love is meant to be. They help to heighten my sensitivities, perceptions and awareness to be able to live my finest moments dangerously exposed beyond the frontier of my knowing. I have long ago discovered that my mind in its search for meaning comes dishearteningly quickly to its frontier of understanding and promptly turns to my heart to carry on beyond my last 'why.' I marvel about how regardless of my inadequacies and fallibilities, my playmates revive in me a fiercely loving heart.

In play there is an unconditional amnesty that carries us beyond the frontiers of fear. This is a journey of a different kind, not within the categories of culture, but out beyond borders undertaken out of love in search of love. Play is the touching of spirits, hearts and bodies in which one playmate gives his or her life into the hands of another. In one instance I am the holder, in the other I am held.

To assume that we are alone and unconnected is an illusion of the most dangerous kind. No matter how much fear, abuse, and aggression are brought into my playground, I continue to turn towards a feeling of wholeness of the human spirit as the only way of preventing humans from forever being mere prisoners of our endless chain of hurt and revenge. When my heart stops, I am exiled from life's current. To be left out of life's play is to be dead, and to be withheld from it for any length of time is to be comatose.

Together we penetrate to the playground that Rumi spoke about where heaven and earth have not yet divided. Coming out to play in this playground we discover our belonging. In these moments of grace the boundaries of species are effaced and the unlimited possibilities of play are allowed to flow as a primary condition written into the contract with life. We give to each other the presence of love and what we receive from each other is the gift of life.

In such a playground there are no enemies, no sides, no fault, no blame, no revenge, no fear, no self defense. Original play is not a matter of fixed technique, not a matter of 'knowing' what to do. Play demands years of practice in that which cannot be practiced, such as the openness of a beginner and a wholehearted intention to give and receive love. In this play there is no need for self-defense. To defend oneself in play is not to play. Self defense is a self-defeating strategy.

Like the child who runs out to engage the fullness of the first day of summer, a radical realization shines from our eyes and roars from our hearts. Such a state of living fully provides us with a sense of belonging that transcends not only how we have thought about our place in the universe, but how the universe itself is organized. This may seem foreign at first, but in time we remember an ancestral intelligence, a yearning for this great belonging, a wild compulsion bubbling to the surface. This is a recovery of original play of a qualitatively different sort. What is involved is a genuine transcendence and not simply a restoration. This difference is described in a Zen poem, *Iron Flute Blown Upside Down:*

> The bellows blew high the flaming forge;
> The sword was hammered on the anvil.
> It was the same steel as in the beginning,
> But how different was its edge.

Genro

Article previously published in a different form in *ZipLines* (Summer, 1999), p8-11.

Contact:

3800 W. Devonshire Ave., Apt. C-78
Tel: (909)925-1496
Fax: (909)925-6123
E-mail: Ofreddybear@aol.com

11. Teaching Kids to Kill

Lt. Col. Dave Grossman

A Case Study: Paducah Kentucky

Michael Carneal, the 14-year-old killer in the Paducah, Kentucky, school shootings, had never fired a real pistol in his life. He stole a .22 pistol, fired a few practice shots, and took it to school. He fired 8 shots at a high school prayer group. He hit 8 different kids with eight shots, five of them head shots and the other three upper torso.

I train numerous elite military and law enforcement organizations around the world. When I tell them of this achievement they are stunned. Nowhere in the annals of military or law enforcement history can I find an equivalent 'achievement.'

Where does a 14-year-old boy who never fired a gun before get the skill and the will to kill? Video games and media violence.

A Virus of Violence

To understand the 'why' behind Jonesboro, Springfield, Pearl, Paducah, and Littleton, we need to first understand the overall magnitude of the problem. The murder rate does not accurately represent the problem. Murder has been held down by the development of ever more sophisticated life saving skills and techniques. A better indicator of the problem is the aggravated assault rate – the rate at which human beings are *attempting* to kill one another. And that has gone up from around 60 per 100,000 in 1957, to over 440 per 100,000 by the mid-1990s.

Even with small downturns in recent years, the violent crime rate is still at a phenomenally high level, and this is true not just in America but worldwide. In Canada, per capita assaults increased almost fivefold between 1964 and 1993, and attempted murder increased nearly sevenfold. According to Interpol, between 1977 and 1993 the per capita assault rate increased nearly fivefold in Norway and Greece, and in Australia and New Zealand it increased approximately fourfold. During the same period it tripled in Sweden, and approximately doubled in: Belgium, Denmark, England-Wales, France, Hungary, Netherlands, and Scotland. In India during this period the per capita murder rate doubled. In Mexico and Brazil violent crime is also skyrocketing, and in Japan juvenile violent crime went up 30 percent in 1997 alone.

This virus of violence is occurring worldwide, and the explanation for it has to be some *new* factor that is occurring in *all* of these countries. Like heart disease, there are many, many factors involved in the causation of violent crime, and we should never downplay any of them. But there is only one *new* variable that is present in each of these nations, bearing the exact same fruit in every case, and that is media violence being presented as 'entertainment' for children.

Killing Unnaturally

I spent almost a quarter of a century as an Army infantry officer, a paratrooper, a Ranger, and a West Point psychology professor, learning and studying how we enable people to kill. Most soldiers have to be trained to kill. And we are doing the same thing to our kids, but without the safeguards. According to the head of the American Academy of Pediatrics (AAP) Task Force on Juvenile Violence, 'children are learning to kill from abuse and violence in the home and, most pervasively, from violence as entertainment in television, the movies, and interactive video games.'

Most healthy members of most species have a powerful, natural resistance to killing their own kind. Animals with antlers and horns fight one another, by butting heads. Against other species they go to the side to gut and gore. Piranha turn their fangs on everything, but they fight one another with flicks of the tail. Rattlesnakes bite anything, but they wrestle one another.

When we human beings are overwhelmed with anger and fear our thought processes become very primitive, and we slam head on into that hard-wired resistance against killing. During World War II, we discovered that only 15-20 percent of the individual riflemen would fire at an exposed enemy soldier. You can observe this resistance throughout history, as I have outlined in much greater detail in my book, *On Killing* (which is being used as a textbook worldwide), in my three peer-reviewed encyclopedia entries, and in my entry in the *Oxford Companion to American Military History.*

That is the reality of the battlefield. Only a small percentage of soldiers are able to kill. The rest may be willing to die, but they are not willing to kill. When the military became aware of this, they systematically went about the process of 'fixing' this 'problem.' And fix it they did. By the Korean War around 55 percent of the soldiers were willing to fire to kill. And by Vietnam the rate rose to over 90 percent.

The Methods in This Madness

The training methods the military uses are brutalization, classical conditioning, operant conditioning, and role modeling. I will explain these in the military context and demonstrate how the media does the same thing to our children, but without the safeguards.

Brutalization and Values Inculcation

Brutalization, or 'values inculcation,' is what happens at boot camp. Your head is shaved, you are herded together naked, and dressed alike, losing all vestiges of individuality. You are trained relentlessly in a total immersion environment. This is designed to break down your existing mores and norms and to accept a new set of values. In the end you embrace violence and discipline and accept it as a normal and essential survival skill in your brutal new world.

Something very similar is happening to our children through violence in the media, but instead of 18-year-olds it begins at the age of 18 months. At that age a child can understand and mimic what is on television. But up until they are six or seven years old they are developmentally, psychologically, physically unable to discern the difference between fantasy and reality.

This means that when a young child sees somebody on TV being shot, stabbed, raped, brutalized, degraded, or murdered, to them it is as though it were actually happening. In the end some of them embrace violence and accept it as a normal and essential survival skill in a brutal new world.

On June 10, 1992, the *Journal of the American Medical Association* (JAMA) published a definitive epidemiological study on the impact of TV violence. In nations, regions, or cities where television appears there is an immediate explosion of violence on the playground, and within 15 years there is a doubling of the murder rate. Why 15 years? That's how long it takes for a brutalized two year-old to reach the 'prime crime' years. That's how long it takes before you begin to reap what you sow when you traumatize and desensitize a toddler or a five year-old.

The JAMA concluded that, 'the introduction of television in the 1950s caused a subsequent doubling of the homicide rate, i.e., long-term childhood exposure to television is a causal factor behind approximately one-half of the homicides committed in the United States, or approximately 10,000 homicides annually.' The study went on to state that '...if, hypothetically, television technology had never been developed, there would today be 10,000 fewer homicides each year in the United States, 70,000 fewer rapes, and 700,000 fewer injurious assaults.'

Today the data linking violence in the media to violence in society is superior to that linking cancer and tobacco. The American Psychological Association (APA), the American Medical Association, the AAP, the Surgeon General, and the Attorney General have all made definitive statements about this. When I presented a paper to the American Psychiatric Association's (APA) annual convention in May 2000, the statement was made that: 'The data is irrefutable. We have reached the point where we need to treat those who try to deny it, like we would treat Holocaust deniers.'

Classical Conditioning
Classical conditioning is like Pavlov's dog in Psych 101. The ringing bell was associated with food, and eventually the dog could not hear the bell without salivating.

Early in World War II, the Japanese would make some of their young, unblooded soldiers bayonet innocent prisoners to death. Their friends would cheer them on. Afterwards, all these soldiers were treated to the best meal they had had in months, sake, and to so-called 'comfort girls.' The result? They learned to associate violence with pleasure.

This technique is so morally reprehensible that there are very few examples of it in modern U.S. military training, but the media is doing it to our children. They watch vivid images of human death and suffering and they learn to associate it with: laughter, cheers, popcorn, soda, and their girlfriend's perfume.

After the Jonesboro shootings, one of the high schoo told me about her students' reaction when she told t someone had shot a bunch of their little brothers, sisters, and cousins in the middle school. 'They laughed,' she told me with dismay, 'they laughed.' We have raised a generation of barbarians who have learned to associate vivid depictions of human death and suffering with pleasure.

Operant Conditioning

The third method the military uses is operant conditioning, a very powerful procedure of stimulus response training. A benign example is the use of flight simulators to train pilots, or children in fire drills.

When the fire alarm is set off, the children learn to file out of the school in orderly fashion. One day there is a real fire and they are frightened out of their little wits, but they do exactly what they have been conditioned to do and it saves their lives.

The military and law enforcement community have made killing a conditioned response. In World War II we taught our soldiers to fire at bullseye targets, but that training failed miserably in preparing our soldiers for combat. We have no known instances of any soldiers being attacked by bullseyes.

Now soldiers learn to fire at realistic, man-shaped silhouettes that pop up in their field of view. That is the stimulus. The conditioned response is to shoot the target and then it drops. Stimulus-response, stimulus-response, repeated hundreds of times. Later, when they are in combat and somebody pops up with a gun, reflexively they will shoot and shoot to kill. Of the shooting on the modern battlefield, 75 to 80 percent is the result of this kind of stimulus-response training.

If we are a little troubled by that, then we should be far more troubled by the fact that every time a child plays an interactive point-and-shoot video game, they are learning the exact same conditioned reflex and motor skills. In his national presidential radio address on April 24, 1999, shortly after the Littleton High

School massacre, President Clinton stated that: 'A former lieutenant colonel and professor, David Grossman, has said that these games teach young people to kill with all the precision of a military training program, but none of the character training that goes along with it.'

The result is ever more homemade pseudo-sociopaths who kill reflexively and show no remorse. Our kids are learning to kill and learning to like it. The most remarkable example is the Paducah, Kentucky, school shooting outlined at the beginning of this article. Eight shots, eight hits, on eight different milling, scrambling, screaming kids. Five of them were head shots. Where did he get this phenomenal skill? Well, there is a $130-million lawsuit against the video game manufacturers, currently working itself through the appeals system, claiming that the violent video games, the murder simulators, gave that mass murderer the skill and the will to kill.

In July 2000, at a bipartisan, bicameral Capitol Hill conference in Washington, D.C., the AMA, the APA, the AAP and the American Academy of Child and Adolescent Psychiatry (AACAP) issued a joint statement saying that 'viewing entertainment violence can lead to increases in aggressive attitudes, values and behavior, particularly in children. Its effects are measurable and long lasting. Moreover, prolonged viewing of media violence can lead to emotional desensitization toward violence in real life... Although less research has been done on the impact of violent interactive entertainment [such as video games] on young people, preliminary studies indicate that the negative impact may be significantly more severe than that wrought by television, movies or music.'

Role Models

In the military you are immediately confronted with a role model: your drill sergeant. He personifies violence, aggression, and discipline. (The discipline, and the fact that it is being done to adults, is the safeguard.) Along with military heroes, such as John Wayne, Audey Murphy, Sergeant York and Chesty Puller, these violent role models have always been used to influence young, impressionable teenagers.

Today the media are providing our children with role models, not just in the lawless sociopaths in movies and in TV shows, but in the transformation of these schoolyard killers into media celebrities.

In the 1970s we learned about 'cluster suicides,' in which TV reporting of teen suicides was directly responsible for numerous copycat suicides of other teenagers. Because of this research, television stations today generally do not cover suicides. But when the pictures of teenage killers appear on TV, the effect is exactly the same. Ask yourself this: If there are children willing to kill themselves to get on TV, are there children willing to kill your child to get on TV?

Thus we get the effect of copycat, cluster murders that work their way across America like a virus spread by the six o'clock local news. No matter what someone has done, if you put their picture on TV, you have made them a celebrity and someone, somewhere, will emulate them. This effect is greatly magnified when the role model is a teenager, and the effect on other teens can be profound.

After the Jonesboro shootings, the Japanese reporters kept asking American reporters, 'Why do you keep putting those killers on TV? Don't you know that this will inspire other kids to do the same thing?' In Japan, Canada, and many other democracies around the world, it is a punishable, criminal act to place the names and images of juvenile criminals in the media, because they know that it will result in other tragic deaths. The media has every right and responsibility to tell the story, but do they have a 'right' to glorify the killers by presenting their visual images on TV?

Unlearning Violence

On the night of the Jonesboro shootings, clergy and counselors were working in small groups in the hospital waiting room, comforting the groups of relatives and friends of the 15 shooting victims. Then they noticed one woman who had been sitting alone silently.

A counselor went up to the woman and discovered that she was the mother of one of the girls who had been killed. She had no friends, no husband, no family with her as she sat in the hospital, alone and stunned by her loss. 'I just came to find out how to get my little girl's body back,' she said. But the body had been taken to Little Rock, 100 miles away, for an autopsy. Told this, in her dazed mind her very next concern was, 'I just don't know how we're going to pay for the funeral. I don't know how we can afford it.' That little girl was truly all she had in all the world, and all she wanted to do was wrap her body in a blanket and take her home.

Some people's solution to this problem is 'If you don't like it, then just turn it off.' If that is your only solution to this problem, then come to Jonesboro, my friend, and tell this mother how this would have kept her little girl safe.

Another possible option to deal with violent crime infringes on civil liberties. We can oppress minorities, take away the freedoms of adults, and extensively regulate our society. One thing that a police state can always truthfully claim is that they can make the streets 'safe.' And if we don't get a grip on violent crime I fear that this is exactly what will happen. But perhaps we can consider regulating what the violence industry is selling to kids, carefully controlling the sale of visually violent imagery to children, while *still* permitting free access to *adults,* just as we do with guns, pornography, alcohol, tobacco, sex and cars.

Fighting Back: Education, Legislation, Litigation

We need to make progress in the fight against child abuse, racism, and poverty, and in rebuilding our families. Work is needed in all these areas, but there's a new front – taking on the producers of media violence. The solution strategy that I submit for consideration is, 'education, legislation, litigation.'

Simply put, we ought to work toward 'legislation' which outlaws violent video games for children. In July 2000, the city of Indianapolis passed just such an ordinance, and any other city, country or state in America has the right to do the same. There is no Constitutional 'right' to teach children to blow people's heads off at the local video arcade.

We are very close to being able to do to the networks, through 'litigation,' what is being done to the tobacco industry. The day may also be coming when we should be able to seat juries in America who are willing to sock it to the networks in the only place they really understand—their wallets.

Most of all, the American people need to be informed, through a comprehensive 'education' campaign, about what is happening. Every parent in America desperately needs to be warned of the impact of TV and other violent media on children, as we would warn them of some rampant carcinogen. Violence is not a game, it is not fun, it is not something that we let children do for entertainment. Violence kills.

CBS President Leslie Moonves when he was asked if he thought the school massacre in Littleton, Colorado had anything to do with the media. His answer was: 'Anyone who thinks the media has nothing to do with it, is an idiot.' *That* is what the networks are selling. We do not have to buy it. Along with a little legislation and litigation, an educated and informed society can find their way home from the dark and lonely place to which we have traveled.

Lt. Col. Dave Grossman is a retired Army Ranger, West Point psychology professor, and an expert on the psychology of killing. He has testified before the U.S. House and Senate, and his research was cited by the President of the United States in the wake of the Littleton school shootings. He is director of the Killology Research Group in Jonesboro, Arkansas, and has written *On Killing: The Psychological Cost of Learning to Kill in War and Society* (Little, Brown and Co., 1996) and has co-written *Stop Teaching Our Kids to Kill: A Call To Action Against TV, Movie and Video Game Violence,* (Crown/Random House, 1999).

Contact:

E-mail: LtColDaveG@aol.com

Appendix 1:
Alliance for Childhood

'Work with us for children everywhere'

What is the Alliance?

The Alliance for Childhood is a forum for partnerships of individuals or organisations who work together out of respect for childhood in a worldwide effort to improve children's lives.

Aims and Objectives

- **To fight poverty and neglect in all forms**
  Too many children suffer poverty, neglect, abuse and discrimination, undermining the basic human right to a nurtured childhood.

- **To work for better child health, physical and emotional**
  Parents, educators and health care professionals can optimise their support for children by collaborating with each other and sharing their expertise.

- **To prevent commercialism aimed at children**
  Children need protecting from the manipulation of hard selling and advertising until mature enough to make informed choices.

- **To reduce children's growing dependence on electronic media**
  Recent research shows that too much exposure to TV, computer and video games adversely affects children's physical, emotional, social and mental development. By sharing experiences, parents and educators can work together to offer children creative and healthy alternative activities.

- **To improve childcare facilities**
  Working parents need affordable, high quality childcare providing a caring environment with appropriate activities for the very young and an unhurried pace of learning.

- **To promote a play-based Early Years curriculum**
  Experience and research shows that creative play and self-directed activities give children a sound basis for life-long learning and promote healthy emotional and social growth. Too exclusive a focus on early academic skills – particularly through formal instruction – has been shown to hinder this process.

- **To strengthen family life**
  The activities of the alliance promote and support family life in all its forms.

How Does the Alliance work?

The quality of childhood is the shared responsibility of all citizens in a democratic society. The Alliance for Childhood strives to create a focal point for reflection and action by people with vision and devotion who place child education and care within a larger social context.

The Alliance works internationally, nationally and locally through:

- Exchanging information, research and experience to ensure co-ordinated action.
- Promoting research and identifying conditions for healthy child development.
- Creating a network of Alliance partners.
- Collating regular reports from around the world.
- Disseminating information through conferences, publications and the media.
- Working with government agencies to influence change in laws and policies.
- Forming local partnerships to promote the Alliance's aims and objectives amongst parents, child carers, educators, health care professionals and within local government.
- Encouraging joint activities between a range of community-based organisations involving children and adults.

Contact

Belgium
Alliance for Childhood
Lange Lozanastaat 117, B-2018 Antwerp
Tel/fax: (+32) 3 2378710
E-mail: Internatalliance.childhood@online.be

Brazil
Alianca para Infancia
Luiza Lameirao e Ute Craemer
av. Tomas de Souza 552, 05836-350 Sao Paulo
Tel: (+55) 11 585 15370 Fax: (+55) 11 585 11089
E-mail: ascmazul@amcham.com.br
www.sab.org.br/monteazul

Germany

Alliance for Childhood
c/o Internal Waldorf Kindergarten Association
D-70188 Stuttgart, Heubergstraße 18
Tel: (+49) 711 925740 Fax: (+49) 711 925747
E-mail: Inter.waldorf@t-online.de

Sweden

Alliance for Childhood
Dragonvägen 13, S-177675 Järfälla
Tel/fax: (+46) 85835 8516
E-mail: sekretariatet@waldorf.se

Switzerland

Alliance for Childhood
Medical Section, Goetheanum, CH-4143 Dornach
Tel: (+41) 61 706 4290 Fax: (+41) 61 706 4291
E-mail: Med.sektion@goetheanum.ch

United Kingdom

Alliance for Childhood
Kidbrooke Park, Forest Row, E. Sussex, RH19 5JA
Tel: (+44) 1342 822115 Fax: (+44) 1342 826004
E-mail: alliance@waldorf.compulink.co.uk
www.allianceforchildhood.org.uk

United States of America

Alliance for Childhood
PO Pox 444, College Park, MD 20741
Tel: (+1) 301 699 9058 Fax: (+1) 301 779 3272
E-mail: jalmon@erols.com
www.allianceforchildhood.org

Childhood

Childhood is a time for learning about the essentials –
about the heavenly world and the earthly,
about goodness, beauty and truth.

Childhood is a time to be loved and to love –
to express fear and to learn to trust –
to be allowed to be serious and calm
and to celebrate with laughter and joy.

Children have a right to dream,
and they need to grow at their own pace.
They have the right to make mistakes
and the right to be forgiven.

Children need help to develop self mastery,
to transform themselves and bring forth their highest capacities.

Children have a right to be spared violence and hunger
to have a home and protection.
They need to grow up healthily,
with good habits and sound nutrition.

Children need people to respect,
adults whose example and loving authority they follow.
They need a range of experience – tenderness and kindness,
boldness and courage, and even mischief and misbehaviour.

Children need time for receiving and giving,
for belonging and participating.
They need to be part of a community,
and they need to be individuals.

They need privacy and sociability.
They need time to rest and time to play,
time to do nothing and time to work.
They need moments for devotion and room for curiosity.
They need protective boundaries and freedom for creativity.
They need to be introduced to a life of principles,
and given the freedom to discover their own.
They need a relationship to the Earth
to animals and to nature;
and they need to unfold as human beings within the community.

The spirit of childhood is to be protected and nurtured.
It is an essential part of every human being
and needs to be kept alive.

(International Joint Alliance Working Group,
New York 1999)

Appendix 2:
Children have Rights

Humanity owes to the Child the Best it has to Give
This is what it says in the 'Declaration of Rights of the Child', which was adopted unanimously on 20 November 1959 by the General Assembly of the United Nations. In ten principles this declaration lays down the rights to which each child is entitled.

Children have Rights

1   The right to equality, regardless of race, colour, religion, sex or nationality.

2   The right to healthy mental and physical development.

3   The right to a name and a nationality.

4   The right to sufficient food, housing and medical care.

5   The right to special care if handicapped.

6   The right to love, understanding and care.

7   The right to free education, play and recreation.

8   The right to immediate aid in the event of disasters and emergencies.

9   The right to protection from cruelty, neglect and exploitation.

10 The right to protection from persecution and to an upbringing in the spirit of worldwide brotherhood and peace.

Getting in touch with Hawthorn Press

What are your pressing questions about the early years?
The Hawthorn Early Years series arises from parents' and educators' pressing questions and concerns – so please contact us with *your* questions. These will help spark new books, workshops or festivals if there is sufficient interest. We will be delighted to hear your views on our Early Years books, how they can be improved, and what your needs are.

Visit our website for details of the Early Years Series and forthcoming books and events: **www.hawthornpress.com**

Ordering books

If you have difficulties ordering Hawthorn Press books from a bookshop, you can order direct from:

United Kingdom
Scottish Book Source Distribution,
137 Dundee Street, Edinburgh, EH11 1BG
Tel: 0131 229 6800 Fax: 0131 229 9070

North America
Anthroposophic Press c/o Books International,
PO Box 960, Herndon, VA 201 72-0960.
Toll free order line: 800-856-8664
Toll free fax line: 800-277-9747

Other books from Hawthorn Press

Early Years Series

Muddles, Puddles and Sunshine
Your activity book to help when someone has died
Winston's Wish

Muddles, Puddles and Sunshine offers practical and sensitive support for bereaved children. Beautifully illustrated, it suggests a helpful series of activities and exercises accompanied by the friendly character of Bee and Bear.

September 2000; 32pp; 297 x 210mm landscape; colour illustrations; paperback; 1 869 890 58 2

Free to Learn
Introducing Steiner Waldorf Early Years Education
Lynne Oldfield

From the Foreword by
Sally Jenkinson:

'For almost eighty years
in as many different
contexts and cultures,
from the Favelas in Sao
Paulo to the townships
in South Africa, Steiner
Waldorf Education has provided early years care and education
for some of the world's children. Described as 'this most modest
movement' its kindergartens and schools have consistently striven
to give children the highest quality of educational nurturing in
their early years.

Different kindergartens vary according to local need but what
remains constant is a deeply held belief that childhood matters;
that the early years are not a phase of life to be rushed through,
but a stage of tremendous importance needing to be experienced
fully in its own right. Underpinning this book is the conviction
that the child's early learning is profound; that quality of early
experience is every bit as important as quantity. It is a book
which implicitly acknowledges that the way we learn, as well as
what we learn, will set the arrow of our future on its particular
course, for better or for worse.'

160pp; 216 x 138mm; paperback; 1 903 458 06 4

Storytelling with Children
Nancy Mellon

Telling stories awakens wonder and creates special occasions with children, whether it is bedtime, around the fire or on rainy days. Encouraging you to spin golden tales, Nancy Mellon shows how you can become a confident storyteller and enrich your family with the power of story.

Children love family storytelling and parents can learn this practical, magical art. Here are tips and resources you need for:

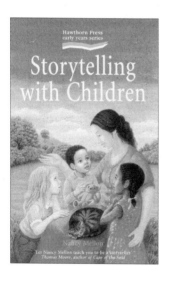

- Creating a listening space
- Using the day's events and rhythms to make stories
- Transforming old stories and making up new ones
- Bringing your personal and family stories to life
- Learning stories by heart using pictures, inner theatre, walk-about, singing the story and other methods
- Finding the tale you want from her rich story-cupboard.

Nancy Mellon is a storyteller who teaches the healing art of storytelling. She runs a School for Therapeutic Storytelling and lives in New Hampshire.

Autumn 2000; 224pp; 216 x 138mm; illustrations; paperback; 1 869 890 02 7

Free Range Education
Ed Terri Dowty

Considering educating your children at home? Then *Free Range Education* will help you make better choices by asking 'what is home education?', 'what are the benefits?', and 'how do you educate at home?' Parents and students describe their approaches to education at home and provide helpful examples, good stories, resources, contacts and information on your rights.

224pp; 216 x 138mm; paperback; 1 903458 07 2

The Genius of Play
Sally Jenkinson

This book is an observation of the tireless imagination of the child when it is allowed to develop naturally, and how this shapes the perceptions of the later adult. It addresses what 'play' is, why it is necessary and its modern difficulties.

Autumn 2000; 128pp; 216 x 138; paperback; 1 903 458 06 4

Birthday Book
Ann Druitt, Christine Fynes-Clinton and Marije Rowling

Everything you need for celebrating birthdays in enjoyable ways. There are suggestions for 'oldies', for teenagers, 18th and 21st parties as well as children's parties. You will find unusual celebrations for those on holiday, ill in bed, at Christmas or for rainy days.

192pp; 246 x 189mm; paperback; 1 903458 01 3

Alliance for Childhood: Brussels Conference 2000 Proceedings: Order form

Dear Reader

If you want to order a copy of Conference Proceedings, please fill in your name and address on the order form and return to Hawthorn Press. The cost will be in the region of £15.00 plus £2.00 p&p.

Name _____

Address _____

_____

_____

Postcode _____ Tel. no. _____

Please return to: Hawthorn Press, Hawthorn House, 1 Lansdown Lane, Stroud, Glos. GL5 1BJ, UK or Fax: (01453) 751138

Name of your organisation, for invoicing purposes:

_____

When we have enough orders to make the publication of an English Proceedings possible, (eg 300-350 orders) we can go ahead with publication in early 2001. See our website for more details.